Why Be
Jewish?

Also by Edgar Bronfman

Why Be Jewish?

A TESTAMENT

Edgar M. Bronfman

SIGNAL
MCCLELLAND
& STEWART

Library and Archives Canada Cataloguing in Publication is available upon request

Published simultaneously in the United States of America by Twelve, a division of the Hachette Book Group, New York, USA.

Library of Congress Control Number is available upon request

ISBN: 978-0-7710-1737-7
ebook ISBN: 978-0-7710-1727-8

Cover design by Christopher Brian King
Tree logo by Marc Friedland / Marc Friedland Couture Communications
Printed and bound in the United States of America

Published by Signal,
an imprint of McClelland & Stewart,
a division of Penguin Random House Canada Limited
www.penguinrandomhouse.ca

1 2 3 4 5   20 19 18 17 16

CONTENTS

FOREWORD

Before I ever had the privilege of meeting Edgar Bronfman, he had already changed my life. At the age of sixteen, I was selected to be one of twenty-five North American Jews in the third class of Bronfman Fellows in Israel. That summer of 1989, as a pluralistic family of "Bronfmanim," we unpacked Jewish texts, traveled the land of Israel, learned from literary and cultural giants, and challenged each other's beliefs. That summer transformed my Jewish identity and inspired me to become a rabbi. I find it somewhat hard to believe that a few decades later I would be invited to write the foreword for what would be Edgar Bronfman's last book. As a young woman, born in South Korea, I was a most unlikely candidate ever to become a rabbi, and I am deeply honored to write a fore-word for the man most responsible for my involvement in the Jewish world. His vision lives on in the many young people whose lives he transformed, and who are finding in Judaism the qualities he so valued: a sense of joy, a love of learning and questioning, and an imperative to leave the world a better place than you found it.

Had I not been a Bronfman Fellow that fateful summer, it is likely that I would be among the growing number of younger Jews who feel disenfranchised from organized Jewish life. The most recent Pew Report on Jewish life (2013) indicates that the fastest-growing identification among younger Jews is "Jews of no religion." This trend falls right in line with larger ones in all American religions. There is an increasing secularization among the younger population, even as many of them identify as being "spiritual" or "seekers." For many Americans of a younger generation, religious life and language have become associated with a more right-leaning political orientation and worldview. God-language is challenging and off-putting, and thereby leads to a rejection of all things religious. Unfortunately, too many Jews don't realize that religion is only one strand in the ever-changing Jewish tapestry.

Edgar Bronfman's *Why Be Jewish?* offers a compelling invitation for younger generations, and Jews of all ages, to take another look at Judaism, irrespective of the religious aspects of the tradition. Edgar describes a substantive and meaningful Jewish identification that does not require a belief in a supreme being to be transformative. He begins his book by recounting how he walked away from his own practice as a young man, and only found his way back when he was almost sixty years old. Like the Talmudic story of Rabbi Akiva, who begins learning the Hebrew alphabet at the age of forty, Edgar exemplified in his own life that it is never too late to become a serious student of our tradition. In his many years of study, he developed a deep appreciation for Jewish texts—the values they embody, the discourse and argumentation they engender, the miracle of our historical Jewish drama—and an abiding love for Jewish people around the world.

Edgar titles the first chapter of his book "Beyond Belief." These two simple words suggest many layers of literal and symbolic meaning. In rabbinic tradition, the Hebrew/Aramaic word *Pardes* refers to an orchard or garden. As an acronym, PRDS is an approach to biblical exegesis, representing four approaches to understanding a text: *pshat* (simple or literal); *remez* (allegorical meaning); *derash* (seek); and *sod* (the mysterious or esoteric).

On a simple or *pshat* level, the book strongly advocates for a Judaism that can be beyond belief—not requiring a belief in God, and yet compelling in its meaning and moral mandates. Edgar also implicitly *drashes*, or comments, on a book of the same title by the preeminent twentieth-century American sociologist of religion, Robert Bellah. *Beyond Belief*, published in 1970, is a collection of Bellah's essays and includes his seminal article "Civil Religion in America." Bellah understood that there could be an embrace of a common American "civil religion" with shared "sacred texts," rituals, holidays, and values independent of a person's chosen religion or religion of birth. Edgar picks up on this theme of a kind of civil or secular religious approach to Judaism, emphasizing those shared aspects enumerated above, as a means of creating a

Judaism and a Jewish community that can be transcendent and unifying, irrespective of your particular belief in God.

On the deepest level, the *sod, Why Be Jewish?* expresses Edgar Bronfman's awe, respect, and deep love for Judaism. This manifesto is a passionate testimonial to his personal journey and to the incredible story of the Jewish people, who against all odds have changed the world. As a rabbi, I was prepared to be a little defensive on reading a book that advocates for a Jewish identity that can be beyond a belief in God. While I acknowledge that one can be a Jew and not believe in God, I have spent my career as a rabbi trying to expand the definition of God from a solely biblical view of an anthropomorphic, omnipotent God to experiences of the divine that can be understood in the wonder of creation, in moments of moral courage, and in extraordinary acts of human goodness.

Edgar beautifully frames this challenge with compelling language that completely resonates with the desire to understand the divine in an expanded, rational way. He posits that while he does not believe in a supernatural God, he practices a Judaism that encourages us to aspire to "godliness": the true, the good, and the beautiful. He does not seek to strip Judaism and our approach to the world to what he calls an "antiseptic atheism that bleaches away all natural wonder and beauty." Instead, with humility, he acknowledges the mystery beyond our comprehension. He embraces a new secularism that includes an appreciation for the natural miracles of the world and the "moral miracles" that are reflected in amazing acts of human kindness and decency. I am grateful for Edgar's reasoned articulation of a form of secularism rich with the kind of godliness that Judaism aspires to bring to the world.

With a stated life mission of helping to keep more liberal strands of Judaism alive and thriving, Edgar takes on the challenge of formulating "secular tenets" of Judaism that would compel a rational yet spiritually seeking young Jew to engage in Jewish life. He picks twelve tenets, using a number symbolic of the twelve tribes of Israel, and articulates what he sees as the highest values of our tradition. These include welcoming the stranger, conducting business ethically, asking questions, and revering godliness. Every one of these tenets is an active verb, representing things to do, not things to believe.

Throughout the book, Edgar walks us through these secular tenets and other major ideas in Jewish life. He fleshes out their meaning for our own lives and offers proof texts from our tradition that are gleaned over his many years of study with some of the greatest teachers in the Jewish world. He weaves in narrative from his own journey with honesty, poignancy, and the passion of the converted. True to his larger message, he quotes wisdom not only from the Jewish world but from some of the most important thinkers in the larger philosophical and scientific domain. By mining the richness of these sources and the depth of his own experience, he makes a compelling case for the meaning and transcendence of a secular Judaism that is steeped in deep moral values, authentic Jewish texts, and a focus on deed over creed or dogma.

Perhaps the most important message of the book is in the life of the messenger itself. *Why Be Jewish?* reflects the views, feelings, and ideas that became Edgar Bronfman's lifework and his most important legacy to the Jewish community. In the most significant ways, Bronfman embodied the central message of his book: to keep Judaism alive not just through words and beliefs, but through action. With his engagement in weekly study with teachers representing Jews across the spectrum, he lived the Jewish value of continued intellectual inquiry and questioning. He championed social justice causes and helped to repair the world with his many and varied philanthropic initiatives, which received his generous resources as well as his own energy and time.

Edgar not only challenged each Jew to interpret and question Judaism and make it his or her own, but he demonstrated this in his own efforts to craft a meaningful Jewish practice. *The Bronfman Haggadah*, published in 2013, retells the Passover story and the miracle of our redemption without a supernatural God at the center. This thoughtful and beautifully presented work includes Edgar's original language and the artwork of his wife, Jan Aronson.

I would venture that Edgar's work on the Haggadah may have inspired the final chapter of *Why Be Jewish?*: "A Lesson in Leadership." He gleans lessons of character, initiative, and moral courage from the biblical hero of the Exodus narrative. He focuses on Moses not as a manager but as a man with brilliance and flaws, who ultimately was able to transform the world through his leadership. And now the fruits of Edgar Bronfman's own leadership are being felt in many corners of the Jewish world, as so many of the young people he has influenced have gone out into the world to revitalize Jewish learning, to become Jewish professionals, and to work for social justice, compelled by their own Jewish identification and values.

A striking example can be found in the chapter "Here and Now," which focuses on the Jewish call for justice and *tzedakah*. Edgar highlights the work of Idit Klein, Taylor Krauss, and Jeremy Hockenstein, amazing young Jews who are working in justice fields as diverse as LGBT rights, the Rwandan genocide, and poverty in Cambodia. Not only are these all outstanding examples of Jews whose mandate for their work comes from their own sense of Jewish identity, but they all are "Bronfmanim," alumni of the Bronfman Fellowships that Edgar Bronfman began more than twenty-five years ago. In a very real sense, Edgar's vision has had a ripple effect in the larger world. The actions of these Bronfmanim powerfully convey what Jews should stand for and how we can transform and repair the world. I cannot imagine a more powerful testament to Edgar's message.

Throughout *Why Be Jewish?*, Edgar states in many ways that he does not believe in a supernatural God, but that the God he experiences in the world can be found in the actions of human beings. We cannot merely pray for God to feed all who are hungry or to help those most vulnerable in society. We must be the change we want to see in the world. And we cannot use guilt, threats, or even prayer to keep Judaism alive. We must make the case for why Judaism is worth preserving in our own time, in our own lives.

Edgar Bronfman was one of those "angels" (not a word he would like, but one I use metaphorically!) who, in my view, helped to accomplish God's divine work here on earth. *Why Be Jewish?* is his strongest and most beautiful articulation of what it means to pursue this work. Throughout its pages, he pushes us to help repair our troubled world, armed with the strength, wisdom, and optimism of our Jewish tradition. Edgar Bronfman's impact on the Jewish world is beyond belief, and I am confident his message will reverberate for generations to come.

—*Angela Warnick Buchdahl*

INTRODUCTION

The pursuit of knowledge for its own sake, an almost
fanatical love of justice, and the desire for personal
independence—these are the features of the Jewish tradition which make me thank my stars I belong to it.

—Albert Einstein, *The World as I See It*

What we have loved Others will love
And we will teach them how.

—William Wordsworth, *The Prelude*

As a young man, I walked away from my rudimen-
tary practice of Judaism. Throughout much of my adult life I
spurned religious practice and raised my children in a home
where Judaism was almost entirely absent. While I fought
Jewish persecution, my identity was shaped by a sense of
belonging to a specific ethnic group rather an attachment to
the Jewish tradition.

Fortunately, around age sixty that all changed, as I began
a journey through the deep, rich, and fascinating world of
Judaism. Despite my own skepticism about traditional belief

in God, I have found much in my heritage that brings meaning and value. I wrote this book to encourage others, particularly those of a younger generation who are doubters like me, to embark on this journey and to create a Jewish practice of their own.

Like all grand journeys, mine was set in motion by several incidents.

The first occurred in Moscow in the 1970s where, as president of the World Jewish Congress, I was lobbying on behalf of Soviet Jewry during the holiday of *Simchat Torah*, the celebration of the end of the reading of the Torah and the beginning of the next reading cycle. Though Judaism had been officially banned in the Soviet Union for the previous seventy-five years, these Jews were celebrating nonetheless. As I looked on, I marveled over the fact that despite years of religious suppression in the Soviet Union, they still celebrated this joyful holiday. My curiosity was piqued: What is it about Judaism that has kept it alive when so many other civilizations have disappeared?

On the aircraft home, my traveling companion, Rabbi Israel Singer, pulled a little book out of his pocket, opened it, and started reading. After ten minutes, he put the book away. Intrigued, I asked him what he was reading. He said that it was one of the sixty-three tractates of the more than six thousand pages of the Talmud. I asked him how long it would take to get through the whole thing.

"About seven and a half years," he answered.

"Wow!" I said. "So tell me, what did it say today?"

"You don't care about what it said."

"Look! We're on the plane. We have nothing to do for hours, so why not tell me what you're reading?"

Singer sighed. "Torah tells you that if you have an ox that gores three people, you must kill the ox. But it doesn't tell you what to do with the remains of the ox, which has value. The Talmud tells us who gets what."

My first reaction was that this was pretty arcane stuff. But in the next moment, I realized it wasn't arcane at all. I suddenly realized that my distant ancestors were exploring systems of justice and equitable distribution long before the system of torts had been developed. I asked, "Are there a lot of complex questions and situations like this in the Talmud?"

"It's full of such questions and situations," he replied. Intrigued, I resolved to learn more about this ancient book of wisdom. I decided to read the Torah too, starting with the very first word of Genesis. I worked with the Stone edition, which was illuminated with wonderful commentary, and whenever I had a question, I would email a message to Singer and we would discuss the text in detail. I also had passionate discussions with the rabbi, scholar, and activist Arthur Herzberg, especially about the lives of King David and King Solomon. These energetic exchanges were my first taste of what would become a vital and sustaining practice of Jewish text study.

About this same time, I met my current wife, the artist Jan Aronson. Jan came from a nonobservant but nonetheless committed New Orleans Jewish family. We had both been divorced before and were very aware of what we wanted in a marriage and how to protect it. An important element for Jan was to create a Jewish home, something she had not done in her first marriage.

Given my rising curiosity about Judaism, I was willing to go along. To my surprise, when she lit the *Shabbat* candles on Friday night and said the ancient prayer, I found myself deeply moved. Perhaps it was hearing the Hebrew of my childhood—a language that once sounded rote and deadening to my ear, but now was magically alive. Or maybe it was the peaceful feeling the twin flames ushered into our home or the graceful ballet of Jan's hands as they circled the candles, welcoming the spirit of *Shabbat*. These feelings were repeated when I raised my silver *kiddush* cup and sang the blessing over the wine, beginning with, "*Yom HaShishi*…the sixth day."

Today, I am grateful for these various events that inspired my Jewish journey—a journey that, step by step, has led me from a dismissive attitude toward Judaism to one of joyous embrace. During the course of this journey, I discovered that even for a nonreligious Jew like me who rejects the notion of a supernatural God acting on our behalf, Judaism remains an immensely rich enterprise.

Not surprisingly, the more I learned about this ancient

tradition—from its celebration of rebels and emphasis on ethics, questioning, community, and family, to its beautifully crafted holidays and life-cycle events that provide us with an intense framework for living—the more I wanted to know. Like an orchard, Judaism has deep roots and provides essential nourishment. Having eaten of its fruits, I am a better person, and as a result, my home is a more interesting, more loving, and more understanding place.

In my parents' generation being Jewish was not a choice: It was a condition of life, defined by the ties of history and community that endured among immigrants, and by the anti-Semitism that was still prevalent. Now young Jews can choose whether or not to hold on to their Jewish practice, which to many can seem antiquated, patriarchal, and distant from their own lives and values. As a Jewish leader I am well aware that unless we win over our disinterested Jews, a nearly four-thousand-year-old civilization of tremendous beauty and worth could end up in the dustbin of history. Another possibility that troubles me is that due to a high birth rate among the ultra-Orthodox, this great civilization could be redefined by those have chosen to turn their backs on a good part of the modern world. Though the Jewish religion has always contained a strain of zealotry, it has an even more powerful tradition of openness, inclusiveness, and questioning.

I feel that Judaism is too precious a thing to lose. My feelings on this topic run so deep that my words sometimes feel like a *cri de coeur*, an impassioned plea of the heart. For the past quarter of a century, much of my advocacy has been in service of imperiled Jews and Jewish communities around the world. More recently, this desire has broadened to include the saving of cultural Judaism itself. Given the high assimilation rates in North America, part of my task is to persuade disinterested Jews to take another look.

What I envisioned for this book was not a detailed narrative of Jewish belief or practice. Oceans of ink have already been spilled on that topic, and even if this were not the case, I lack the authority to write comprehensively on such topics, as I am not a rabbi, scholar, or educator. However, in my roles as a Jewish activist and philanthropist, I have been steeped in Judaism for more than twenty-five years, and through this involvement I developed a deep and absorbing love for our traditions and people. It is this passion that I seek to pass along.

My aim in writing this book is to encourage others to take another look at their tradition and craft a practice of their own, one that need not include belief in a traditional God. Some might say that my approach is idiosyncratic at best, heretical at worst. But Judaism is an organic religion that has always grown and changed in response to social, political, and intellectual conditions and orientations.

An emphasis on creativity and adaptation can be found throughout Jewish sources. In a story from the Talmud, God grants Moses' request to travel into the future, where he enters a famous second-century learning center. At the front of the class, the revered sage, Rabbi Akiva, is expounding on a law. During the lecture, however, Moses becomes hopelessly confused; he simply can't follow the rabbi's lesson. When the teaching is over, a student asks the scholar to identify the source of the law under examination. "It is a law given to Moses at Sinai," the sage replies. Hearing this, Moses lets loose a sigh of relief (*Menachot* 29b).

The story suggests that instead of being ironclad law, the Torah is subject to creative reinterpretation. Though the Bible tells us that Moses received the Torah at Mount Sinai, the sages emphasize that it is the responsibility of future generations to interpret its meaning. That the law can have meanings beyond its letter causes Moses to sigh with relief, not despair.

Similarly, another Talmudic passage tells us that when God gave the Torah to the people of Israel, he gave it to them in the form of wheat and flax so they could make it into food and garments (*Seder Eliyahu Zuta*). This analogy too suggests that our tradition only comes to life with imaginative treatment. Our sacred books are the raw material, not the finished product.

Today, there are many vibrant efforts to reimagine Judaism and create new ways of connecting to Jewish community. The Samuel Bronfman Foundation, in partnership with the Natan Fund and Jumpstart, decided to examine some of these start-up initiatives in a study called *The Jewish Innovation Economy*. We soon discovered that these revitalization efforts were far more than a fringe phenomenon. Like the members of the *Haskalah* movement in eighteenth- and nineteenth-century Europe, today's change-makers are seeking new ways to combine Jewish customs, beliefs, and traditions with secular realities. Fortunately for the nonreligious among us, many of the new modes of Jewish practice don't require synagogue attendance, belief in a personal God, or exacting observance of traditional rituals.

My own Jewish journey has been a process of creating for myself a Jewish practice that is relevant and enriching. It has been shaped in part by wide reading of traditional Jewish sources and of history, literature, and philosophy. I quote from and reflect on these sources throughout this book.

Most important, my journey was guided by many remarkable teachers. These include learned rabbis and professors, but also students I met through my involvement in Hillel International, alumni of the Bronfman Fellowships (the program that I began to cultivate a diverse cadre of Jewish leaders), and my own grandchildren. I share many of their words throughout the book. In doing so, I hope to inspire others to live by the lines from the Talmud that the Bronfman Fellows study as the beginning of their learning experience: "Make for yourself a teacher, and acquire for yourself a friend" (*Pirkei Avot* 1:6). To do this—on terms that are very much your own but rooted in Jewish tradition, in ways that allow you to travel your own path with the support of others—is an undertaking whose value is beyond measure.

Part I

Part I

CHAPTER 1

Beyond Belief

I believe in Spinoza's God, who reveals Himself in the
lawful harmony of the world, not in a God who concerns
Himself with the fate and the doings of mankind.

—Albert Einstein

To young jews who consider themselves secu-
lar, belief in God might seem a prerequisite for Jewish practice. In my own journey, I have explored the meaning of
secular Judaism and the many questions that are raised when
these two words stand side by side.

A key insight for me came from a religious source: Rabbi
Harold Schulweis, the longtime spiritual leader of Temple
Valley Beth Shalom, a Conservative synagogue in Encino,
California. In a conversation with Rabbi Schulweis, I
explained that while I define myself as secular, I am not comfortable calling myself an atheist: In the face of the complexity of the universe, I don't want to assert that I can be sure

of anything. How do I describe the beauty I feel when I hear the harmonies of Tchaikovsky's Violin Concerto in D major or experience the architectural grandeur of Bach, when I take in a landscape bathed in light or see the unbridled joy of children at play? Something inside me stirs that I cannot describe or define. To do so would be like picking off the petals of a rose to explain the flower. As magnificent as reason is, it would be hubris to think we can, through our limited senses, ever know or understand the whole.

Rabbi Schulweis introduced me to the term "godliness" to describe this sense of wonder and mystery. While I reject the notion of a supreme being who can influence our lives, a notion that is undeniably central to some modes of Jewish practice, I find most compelling a Jewish emphasis on the difficulty of comprehending the universe, of taking in the grandeur of creation.

This is a point strikingly made in Job, one of the books of the Hebrew Bible. Job, as the author tells us, was a righteous man who suffered unspeakable horror. In page after page of brilliant poetry, Job calls out to God, seeking an explanation for the misery inflicted upon him. Finally, after a long silence, God responds in a series of questions that underscore the limits of human understanding. In a catalog of images, God asks:

Where were you when I laid the earth's foundations?
Speak if you have understanding....

Who closed the sea behind doors
When it gushed forth out of the womb?...
Have you ever commanded the day to break,
Assigned the dawn its place?...
Have you penetrated to the sources of the sea?...
Have you penetrated the vaults of snow?...
By what path is the west wind dispersed,
The east wind scattered over the earth?...
Can you tie cords to Pleiades
Or undo the reins of Orion?...
Who is wise enough to give an account of the heavens?
Who can tilt the bottles of the sky,
Whereupon the earth melts into a mass,
And its clods stick together? (38:4–38)

Blown away by the beauty of those lines? I am. And they are just a sampling of God's lengthy recital of the world's unfathomable workings and wonders. Job quickly learns that despite his attempts to penetrate the great mystery of existence God describes, his senses are simply too limited to grasp the astonishing complexity of the universe.

The miracles that happen in our world belong to the natural order of things—the sun rising and setting, the song of a bird, a heart beating. There are also miracles created by human beings, from jets streaking through the skies to telescopes that imprint distant galaxies on our eyes. The kind of Judaism I envision embraces miracles such as these and, just as important, what I call "moral miracles": the amazing acts of human goodness, caring, and courage that happen every day, everywhere.

As a secular Jew, I don't pray to a supernatural God. But the idea of godliness helps me to see prayer in a new way: as an opportunity to express my wonder and gratitude in the face of the beauty and mystery of the universe. The Jewish tradition has a blessing known as the *shehecheyanu*, which means, literally, "who has given us life." This prayer is recited at beginnings—at the start of holidays and new seasons—or whenever we experience special events or something that brings us joy. This kind of acknowledgment reminds me of the goodness in my life, and also removes me from the incessant self-focus on my own problems and issues, something to which we humans are all prone.

The Jewish tradition, which is intensely focused on life, has developed an impressive list of things to be thankful for: seeing a rainbow, hearing the rumble of thunder, spotting a flash of lightning, seeing a large mountain, or coming upon a rushing river. The tradition lists many other things, some quite amusing, that are cause for thanksgiving, such as eating a piece of new or unusual fruit, seeing an unusual-looking animal, and acquiring a new suit of clothing. Geraldine Brooks, a Pulitzer Prize–winning novelist who converted to Judaism without believing in God, describes her own practice of appreciation in this reflection published in *Moment* magazine:

Reciting the ancient Hebrew blessings encourages me to notice the small gifts of daily life—the dew on the grass, the new moon, the swift grace and subtle hues of sparrows. Slow down, take a minute, bless the bread and be grateful. This, I tell myself, is what Jews do.

Like Brooks, I find for myself the moments and sensations that inspire me to give thanks. I love the smell of cut wood, so whenever I catch a whiff of that fine, fresh scent, I give thanks to the tree that provided me with this experience. Another pleasure? The silky coat of my wife's dog, a Doberman named Hera. As I run my hand across her sleek neck, I thank her for providing me with tactile delight.

I have also practiced the concept of *shehecheyanu* when lunching with two of my grandchildren, Hannah and Eli. Both in their midtwenties, Hannah and Eli could not be more different by outward appearances. A warm and bright soul, Hannah lives a downtown bohemian life and is involved with the beauty and fashion industries, making her mark as an entrepreneur and DJ. Eli lives in a world of hedge fund managers, investment, and banking. When we meet for lunch, he wears a suit and tie. And yet these two first cousins are the closest of friends, and while they agree on little else in life— from clothes to politics—they share a love of Jewish food. As we nosh and talk, I sometimes pause and silently thank them for being in my life, and for providing me with an opportunity to carry on a tradition started many years ago by my Gramps, who used to take me out for deli lunches. I also give thanks for the fact that unlike in Montreal in the 1930s, the stigma attached to eating Jewish foods in twenty-first-century America has all but vanished.

To call attention to these moments in life is a great habit to develop. It helps us dwell on the positive. Not coincidentally, the more I quietly express my appreciation for the people and things in my life, the more connected I feel to life itself. This is right in line with recent research in the field of neuroplasticity, in which neuroscientists are beginning to validate what the ancient Hebrews knew all along: Consciously concentrating on the good, the true, and the beautiful can restructure the brain in positive ways.

The best sort of prayer is not only an expression of gratitude but a form of ethics in action. In his famous essay "No Religion Is an Island," Rabbi Abraham Joshua Heschel described participating in the Selma civil rights marches as a spiritual experience:

> For many of us the march from Selma to Montgomery was about protest and prayer. Legs are not lips and walking is not kneeling. And yet our legs uttered songs. Even without words, our march was worship.

Rabbi Schulweis, a former pupil of Rabbi Heschel, points out in a *Yom Kippur* sermon that this concept of prayer has a biblical root. When Moses is confronted by pursuing Egyptian warriors and a threatening sea, he prays to God, asking God to do his battle. God replies, "Why do you pray to me? Speak to the people and go forth." Schulweis interprets this to mean that "prayer is not meant to move God—prayer is meant to move you and me, to move the Godliness in you and me, and to move us out of the pew and into the marketplace, out of our designated seats, into the world."

I couldn't agree more.

———

What principles can guide a Jewish practice that moves beyond belief? Without the idea of adherence to divine commandments as a starting point, the question of what a Jewish practice should entail can be overwhelming. As an individual, how does one choose what is important from the immense tradition that has been debated and expounded upon by countless scholars and sages? If our tradition is to find vitality among a new generation, individual Jews and seekers must have the courage to do just that.

To help those just beginning on this journey, I decided to create a list of the principles that have guided my own secular Jewish practice. With the goal of limiting the number of items on this list, I dug through Jewish history, art, and culture in search of a symbolic number, like the seven branches on the *menorah* or the Five Books of Moses. Finally, I fixed on the number twelve, to represent the twelve gems on the *hoshen*, or breastplate worn by the high priests of ancient Israel.

According to the account in Exodus, each of the twelve precious stones was engraved with one of the names of the twelve tribes of Israel. In today's fractured and fractious Jewish world, this symbol of unity held great appeal for me, with many tribes sharing one space. We are all one people, and my great hope is that a more civil discourse will replace the wars going on between Jewish denominations and communities. The image of the shield also appealed to me. Encouraging secular Jews to discover their traditions and create their own practice is a form of protection, helping keep more liberal strains of Judaism from withering away.

Once I established the number of tenets I would include, I set to work. My only rule was that everything on my list must be extrapolated from Jewish text, history, or tradition. All the principles on the list are written in verb form, specifying, with the Jewish emphasis on deed over creed, that these are things to do, not things to believe:

Revere godliness: the true, the good, and the beautiful.

Ask questions.

Commit to repairing the outer and inner world.

Perform acts of loving-kindness.

Assist society's weakest members.

Champion social justice and environmental causes.

Welcome the stranger.

Engage with Jewish traditions, texts, philosophy, history, and art.

Study and strive for excellence in the humanities and other
   secular fields.
Promote family and community.
Embrace key Jewish holidays and life-cycle events.
Conduct business ethically.

The twelve principles on my list are woven through the
chapters that follow, which describe a practice of Judaism that
does not depend on a supreme being. They are intended not as
articles of faith, but as a distillation of the elements of Judaism
that I see as most valuable.

Some of the concepts on my list are frequently emphasized
in Jewish education, like promoting family and community
and embracing Jewish holidays and life-cycle events; others,
like striving for excellence in secular fields, might be less so.
My list highlights the importance of texts, by which I mean
the Torah and the Talmud, but also Jewish history, literature,
and philosophy. I remain convinced that without engagement
with our texts, we can easily end up with an eviscerated kind
of Judaism.

That's why I am so eager for all Jews to gain knowledge of
our textual heritage. And though deep diving is best, even a
dip in the waters of this profound pool of knowledge can yield
great value. As the French mime Étienne Decroux is said to
have quipped, "One pearl is better than a whole necklace of
potatoes." Unfortunately, our texts have traditionally been
under the monopoly of the most religiously oriented members

of the community. The Jewish library belongs to all, whether observant or nonobservant. That's why I am so happy to see the strides being made to secularize the study of Jewish texts, both in North America and in Israel.

Judaism does not demand belief. Instead, it asks us to practice intense behaviors whose purpose is to perfect ourselves and the world. Just as Moses brought down the tablets of the law from the mountaintop, Judaism, through its emphasis on ethics, morality, and human relationships, brings the divine to earth. That is the heart of Jewish spirituality. And it beautifully complements the view of those who, like me, don't believe in traditional notions of God.

In the end, each of us must find our own truth. One of the best ways of ferreting out that truth, or set of truths, is to ask questions. If you don't get the answer you seek, ask again. Don't be afraid to challenge the powers that be. This asking of questions and the willingness to responsibly stand up to the status quo is a very Jewish thing to do.

CHAPTER 2

Question Authority

Nothing is more dangerous than a dogmatic worldview—
nothing more constraining, more blinding to innovation,
more destructive of openness to novelty.

—Stephen Jay Gould, *Dinosaur in a Haystack:*
Reflections on Natural History

SOME MONTHS BACK, A YOUNG FRIEND TOLD ME THAT
he no longer believed in the God of the Bible. The whole idea,
in fact, struck him as ridiculous. Why would such a powerful
force care about the personal problems of billions of people? If
God were perfect, why would children die of hunger or leu-
kemia? Why would animals suffer? Why would the elderly be
neglected? Why would natural disasters destroy the lives of so
many thousands of innocent people? And why would so many
undergo the ravages of cancer and other horrible diseases?
No form of theodicy—the defense of God's goodness in the
face of evil—worked for him. Moreover, he could no longer

tolerate the many rules and rituals of traditional Judaism or what struck him as a mechanical kind of observance.

When he shared these views with his rabbi, he received the kind of authoritative, narrow response that is becoming increasingly common in ultra-Orthodox circles. He was informed that Judaism shorn of transcendence and divine redemption was a kind of Judaism manqué—a Judaism with something missing. In case the young man didn't get it, the rabbi spelled it out even more clearly: The only authentic or true Jews were those who believed in the personal God of the Hebrew Bible and understood that exacting observance was a fundamental requirement.

I quickly assured him that nothing could be more distant from the truth. Far from being a threat, spiritual, intellectual, and moral dissent has always been one of the pillars of Judaism, if not the pillar. What has conventionally been considered Jewish—belief in God, following the Torah's commandments, living a life entirely within a strict religious practice—is not binding. This is hardly a new thought. In the classic text *Jerusalem*, Moses Mendelssohn, the German Jewish philosopher whose ideas led to the Jewish Enlightenment of the eighteenth and nineteenth centuries, points out that the Bible does not command Jews to have faith in God:

Among all the prescriptions and ordinances of the Mosaic Law, there is not a single one that says: You shall believe or not believe. They all say: You shall do or not do. Faith is not commanded, for it accepts no other commands than those that come to it by way of conviction. All the commandments of the divine law are addressed to man's will, to his power to act.

Mendelssohn makes a distinction between belief and practice: Practice is commanded, belief is not. Belief is not unimportant to Mendelssohn, but he holds that it must be accepted on the basis of rational conviction. I assured my young friend that not only was his doubt permissible, but that it placed him in the grand tradition of Jewish figures, both biblical and historical, who had wrestled with, questioned, and challenged God and his ways.

Hearing these things, he looked relieved. As he walked away, I wished I'd been told the same things when, at age nineteen, I experienced similar doubts about the validity of Judaism.

Growing up in Montreal in the 1930s, I would sit beside my father in synagogue and watch as he and other men recited Hebrew prayers by rote. There was nothing joyous about their recitation, nor did I sense that they had any connection to the Hebrew they spoke. They were simply doing what was expected. I knew that as a member of the upcoming generation, I would be expected to pray in a similar, disengaged manner.

One day, I asked my father, "How can you know what you're saying when you read so quickly?"

"I was taught to read," he replied.

I paused, mulling over his words. After a minute or so, I said, "Does that mean that when you pray you have no idea what you're saying?"

He replied, "If you want to put it that way."

That's when I walked out of the synagogue.

It wasn't just the rituals that I found intolerable. As with my young friend, the notion of an anthropomorphic, omnipotent, omniscient God—the superstar of Jewish prayer books, holidays, and customs—did not make sense to me. I just couldn't square it with a world rife with poverty and violence.

Of course, had I been more Jewishly educated, I would have understood that the covenant between man and God is only one strand in the richly hued, ever-changing tapestry of Judaism—a strand that is important, but that is only one of many threads. Moreover, I would have realized that questioning, arguing, and even outright rebellion is integral to Judaism. So integral that according to a *midrash*, a story created by the rabbis of the Talmud to interpret the Bible, the Jewish people began with an act of rebellion: Abraham, then known as Avram, smashing the idols in his father's shop. Here is a version of the story:

One day, while Abraham was tending his father's shop, a man entered. "How old are you?" Abraham asked. When the customer replied that he was sixty, Abraham shook his head in amazement. "How tragic that a sixty-year-old man wants to kneel before a one-day-old idol!" The man was ashamed and left.

Another time, a woman entered the shop, carrying a basket of fruit and bread for the idols. When she'd departed, Abraham picked up a hammer and smashed the idols, leaving only the largest one intact. He then placed the hammer in the hands of the standing idol.

"What happened!" his father angrily demanded when he returned and saw the shattered statues.

Abraham pointed to the fruit and bread. "A woman came in with an offering for the idols. After she left, they got into a quarrel over who would eat first. To solve the problem, the biggest idol snatched up a hammer and smashed the others to pieces. As you can see, the hammer is still in his hand."

His father shouted, "Don't be a fool! Idols have no life! They have no minds! They are incapable of doing anything!"

Abraham quietly responded, "No life? No mind? Not capable of doing anything? If that's true, why do you and others worship them?" (Genesis Rabbah 38:13).

Given the importance of idol worship in 1800 BCE Babylon, we need to remember that this was more than an emotional outburst. In the story, Abraham literally smashed apart the power structure of his world. The idea of a benevolent God who was equally available to all—the ruler and the ruled, the rich and the poor, the powerful and the weak—was absolutely revolutionary, especially when viewed against the common practices of the time: propitiating the demands of capricious gods through child sacrifice and other grisly practices. In establishing a covenant—an agreement—between God and people, Abraham initiated the idea that the perfection of the world rests in our own hands. This thinking was far removed from almost all preceding political systems, which cast ordinary human beings in the role of servants to indifferent gods and powerful rulers.

Nor was this the last of Abraham's protests. He questions the logic of God himself, incredulous at God's plan to destroy the cities of Sodom and Gomorrah. In Genesis, the first book of the Bible, Abraham asks:

> Will you sweep away the innocent along with the guilty? What if there should be fifty innocent within the city; will you then sweep out the place and not forgive it for the sake of the innocent fifty who are in it? Far be it from you to do such a thing, to bring death upon the innocent as well as the guilty, so that innocent and guilty fare alike. Far be it from you! Shall not the Judge of all the earth do justly? (Genesis 18:23–25)

Remarkably, our tradition suggests that Abraham's reproach is the right thing to do. Even when the perpetrator is God himself, we are invited to stand up, to challenge, to question and even chastise. We meet another questioner in the person of Sarah, Abraham's wife. When God tells her she will conceive a child in her old age, she laughs and says, "Now that I am withered, am I to have enjoyment—with my husband so old?" (Genesis 18:12). While not all biblical characters engage in such defiance—Noah, for instance, does not protest God's decision to destroy most of the world—those who do are often chosen to be leaders of the Jewish people.

Job, a righteous man whose livelihood, health, and then family are destroyed by God, is one of the Hebrew Bible's biggest dissidents, loudest lamenters, and most persistent questioners. At the story's start, Job is blessed. He lives in a spacious home, has ten beautiful children, and his pastures and stables are literally overflowing with animals: seven thousand sheep, three thousand camels, five hundred oxen, and five hundred donkeys, to be exact. But in the span of one day, it all changes. Thieves make off with his oxen, donkeys, and camels. Lightning kills his sheep. Disease blackens his skin, causing it to flake off. If that's not enough misery, all his children die. With little regard for Job's sterling character, God pulverizes this innocent man like a moth.

Job stands up to God, pummeling him with questions, trying to make sense of the suffering heaped upon him. But God does not comfort or assure: Instead, he reminds Job that he is incapable of understanding the mysteries of the universe. And when Job's friends answer with pious platitudes, attributing his punishment to sinful acts, Job scoffs at such foolishness. He persists in his questions, refusing to give up until he has found some meaning in his now painful existence.

Questioning is a chief character trait of Moses, Judaism's most revered prophet. After being assigned the task of leading the Hebrew slaves to freedom, Moses challenges God's wisdom. He also questions God when God seeks to destroy the Israelites for worshipping the golden calf:

> The Lord further said to Moses, "I see that this is a stiff-necked people. Now, let Me be, that My anger may blaze forth against them and that I may destroy them, and make you into a great nation." But Moses implored the Lord his God, saying, "Let not Your anger, O Lord, blaze forth against Your people, whom You delivered from the land of Egypt with great power and with a mighty hand. Let not the Egyptians say, 'It was with evil intent that He delivered them, only to kill them off in the mountains and annihilate them from the face of the earth. Turn from Your blazing anger, and the plan to punish Your people. Remember Your servants, Abraham, Isaac, and Israel, how You swore to them by Your Self and said to them: 'I will make your offspring as numerous as the stars of heaven, and I will give to your offspring this whole land of which I spoke, to possess forever.'" And the Lord renounced the punishment He had planned to bring upon His people. (Exodus 32:9–14)

Moses himself is not spared from the persistent questioning of the people of Israel: throughout his tenure as liberator in chief, he is roundly criticized and challenged, his leadership doubted by the unruly mob of former slaves he leads. And let's not forget Judaism's most famous rabbi—Jesus of Nazareth—a rogue Jew if ever there was one, who sought to straighten out the tragically venal Judaism of his time.

Throughout Jewish history, our greatest leaders and scholars have been those who have challenged received wisdom about the beliefs and practices of traditional Judaism in their quest to break new intellectual and spiritual ground. Three of my heroes are Moses Maimonides (1135–1204), Baruch Spinoza (1632–1677), and Moses Mendelssohn (1729–1786). Maimonides, the medieval Jewish philosopher, scholar, and physician who codified Jewish law and ethics, looked askance at the notion of a personal, interventionist God, proffering instead a God too great to be defined by the human mind. Spinoza, a Dutch Jewish philosopher, was an eloquent believer in a secular, democratic society who alarmed the entire Jewish and Christian clergy by denying the possibility of an eternal soul, and further inflamed the theologians with his idea that God is nature. Moses Mendelssohn, a leading figure of the Jewish Enlightenment (*Haskalah*), rejected the then prevalent idea that there should be an established or state religion. In doing so, he paved the way for the separation of church and state, a concept that eventually became the Establishment Clause of the First Amendment of the U.S. Constitution.

Whether biblical or historical, all these figures and many more show that tough questioning, skepticism, and outright rebellion are at the very heart of Judaism. While Judaism doesn't shy away from taking a stand on what is clearly wrong, it embraces cognitive pluralism, making clear that there are multiple ways of viewing our world and its issues. Argumentation, or spirited debate, is also at the heart of the Talmud, where most often dissenting opinions remain side by side without a judgment on which is correct.

Many Jews, including myself, are not comfortable with the notion of submission or obedience. As Rabbi Harold Schulweis points out in an interview in the magazine *Reform Judaism*, questioning obedience is essential because "throughout history, more atrocities—religious and secular—have been committed in the name of obedience than in the name of disobedience. In the last century alone, some 50 million human beings were systematically slaughtered by 'good,' ordinary people, educated in a culture of obedience, who justified their self-acknowledged cruelty with the mantra: 'We followed the orders of our superiors.'"

Along with the moral benefit of questioning, I believe that the Jewish emphasis on intelligent inquiry, when partnered with its celebration of the restless mind, its embrace of multiple views and voices, and the high value it places on education, might explain the disproportionate number of Jews who have made breakthroughs in science, math, history, literature, business, technology, and other fields. Jewish culture and tradition encourage people to fearlessly question and to boldly stand up to the status quo. Judaism charges us to fiercely engage with the world and to challenge everything and anything for the purpose of improving on imperfect or dysfunctional systems.

Prior to my current philosophical study with the gifted professor Dr. Michah Gottlieb, I took a series of philosophy lessons with a graduate student at New York University named Colin Marshall, who was raised as a Christian. During the course of our study on Spinoza, Colin told me about Naomi, a Jewish girl he'd met. Through Naomi he became interested in Judaism, and in the end he converted because, as he explained to me, "it was the only religion that could accommodate questions."

When I learned of his decision to join our people, I felt a certain *naches*, a Yiddish word for joyful pride usually reserved for one's children. Although Colin was thirty years younger, he taught me yet again what I so loved about Judaism.

In fact, I think questioning is the most profoundly Jewish act in which we can engage. We are a faith that requires questions—a seeming contradiction, but something that gives us a wonderful opportunity to learn and act, not simply believe. As a Jewish leader, I have aspired to follow in the footsteps of Judaism's rebellious heroes by speaking out about the aspects of our Jewish community that seem dull, dysfunctional, or flawed.

Questioning, however, is only one step in the process of making change. To move from an imperfect world to a more perfect one requires a fierce commitment of body and spirit. Happily, many young Jews have taken up the challenge, committing themselves to making change in Jewish life and seeking to build a better world.

CHAPTER 3

Here and Now

Let justice well up like water, righteousness like an unfailing stream.

—Amos 5:24

Study leads to action.

—Babylonian Talmud, Kiddushin 40b

Speak up, judge righteously, champion the poor and the needy.

—Proverbs 31:9

THE VOICES OF OUR TRADITION'S GREAT PROPHETS and teachers consistently sound the same themes: that God demands justice and mercy for all people, and that exploitation of the weak by the powerful is a terrible thing. In story after story, teaching after teaching, law after law, Judaism's great books—the Torah and the Talmud—make this point.

So central is the notion of justice to the Jewish narrative that our people's foundational story was ignited by the reaction of Moses, then a prince of Egypt, to an overseer beating a slave.

The search for justice—the redressing of moral wrongs—is also why the book of Deuteronomy commands us "to remember what Amalek did to you" (25:17). Amalek is the name of the nation that attacked us when we were at our most vulnerable, wandering weak and tired in the desert. I see the purpose of this charge not as urging revenge or everlasting hatred, but as reminding us to empathize with those in a position of weakness and vulnerability.

Judaism emphasizes the here and now, and what Einstein called Judaism's "almost fanatical love of justice" reflects this orientation. The Jewish tradition does not emphasize reward or punishment in an afterlife, but constantly asks us to think, in practical ways, how we can better our lives here on earth and improve the lot of our fellow human beings. This concept is humorously captured in this joke: A rabbi, a Buddhist monk, and a priest are sitting together in a room. All of a sudden the electricity goes out, plunging the room into darkness. The Buddhist monk begins meditating on the inner light. The priest excitedly delivers a sermon on Jesus as the light of the world. The rabbi sighs heavily and goes out to buy a flashlight.

Rabbinic literature is also full of passages and stories that teach us to favor practical action over mystical belief. One, attributed to Rabban Yochanan ben Zakkai, tells us, "If you should have a sapling in your hand when they tell you, 'The Messiah is here, come quickly,' plant the sapling and then go out and greet the Messiah" (Avot d'Rabbi Natan 31b). Another reading might suggest that we focus on the business of living since most messiahs in Jewish history have proved false. Either way, the emphasis in much Jewish thought leans heavily toward the earthly and practical.

In another famous story from the Talmud, Rabbi Shimon Bas Yochai criticizes the streets, bridges, and baths of the Romans, suggesting that the Romans have made all these things to benefit themselves. The rabbi's words reach the governor, and, fearful for his life, the rabbi and his son hide themselves in a cave. Here they study and pray for twelve years, sitting up to their necks in sand to preserve their garments.

Twelve years later, they learn that the emperor has died and that it is safe for them to emerge. But when the rabbi leaves the cave, he is enraged at the sight of a fellow Jew going about his daily life under Roman rule. How can people plow and sow when the Temple has been destroyed? He is so angry that fire shoots from his eyes, consuming everything in his line of sight. God angrily orders the rabbi back to the cave for another twelve months, explaining that he is unfit to live in the world (Shabbat 33b). Even with all its flaws, it is our duty to be in the world, this strange story tells us.

The foundational stories in the Bible send the same message. For Abraham, we learn, hospitality toward guests is even more important than welcoming the divine presence. When three strangers come to Abraham's tent, he breaks off his conversation with God to warmly greet them and bathe their feet. Though he eventually learns that these strangers are angels, he is unaware of their identities when he invites them in.

The Talmud expands upon the idea of Abraham's hospitality. In his tent, tradition tells us, the candles of *Shabbat* are always burning, serving as a beacon for those who pass by. One *midrash* teaches, "All the years that Sarah was alive…the doors of the tent were wide open in every direction….There was blessing in the dough of the bread….There was a light burning from one Shabbat eve to the next Shabbat eve" (Genesis Rabbah 60:16). The burning *Shabbat* candle is a beacon, welcoming weary travelers; the blessing in the dough is the blessing of bread shared.

What informs these texts, and so many others like them, is the idea that Jewish spirituality is pragmatic, practical, and worldly. Yes, Judaism also calls our attention to the beautiful mystery of existence, but not at the expense of solving the problems of the world, the practice of ethical behavior, and the loving-kindness shown toward others.

The idea that we should perform positive actions in the world instead of seeking help from a supernatural God comes to life in this humorous anecdote:

A man is drowning. A helicopter arrives with a dangling rope, but he waves it away, shouting, "I am waiting for God to save me!" After several minutes, a man on a raft appears. Again the drowning man waves the rescuer away, explaining that he is waiting for God. When another boat appears, the drowning man responds in the same way. Minutes later, he loses all strength and starts to sink. He calls out to God, "Why didn't you try to save me!" And God answers, "What are you talking about? I tried three times. I sent a helicopter, a raft, and a boat!"

As everyone knows, jokes hold powerful truths. To me this story suggests that godliness exists in the efforts of human beings to help one another. In not understanding this, the man in our joke really misses the boat!

The Torah and the Talmud not only emphasize the importance of bringing justice into our lives here on earth, but they offer highly specific prescriptions for how to do so. These come in the form of *mitzvoth*, the plural of *mitzvah*, a Hebrew word that translates as "commandment." One does not need to see the *mitzvoth* as divinely authored in order to understand the practical wisdom they offer in governing how we relate to our fellow human beings and to our world.

The most famous *mitzvoth* are the Ten Commandments, but the Torah contains many more. Although there have been many attempts to organize and number the commandments contained in the Torah, the traditional and now commonly accepted number is 613, based on the enumeration by the sage Moses Maimonides. The 613 *mitzvoth* cover enormous ground, from protecting fruit trees to managing anger. Some deal with ritual acts, while others concern themselves with ethical or moral behaviors.

In studying the *mitzvoth*, I have come to understand them as the means by which every individual can guide his or her own actions, much like the concept of "locus of control" in the field of personality psychology. This idea refers to how people perceive the outcome of events. Some see the locus of control in their lives as external to themselves, understanding their life outcomes as defined by outside forces. Others believe that the events in their life derive primarily from their actions. This translates to a greater belief in their ability to create change. Though our sages did not have a name for this concept, they were thousands of years ahead of modern psychology. The *mitzvoth*, laid out in minute detail in the Torah and expanded upon in the Talmud, bring the center of action to human beings, giving them the responsibility, and the tools, to create meaningful lives for themselves.

The spirit of the *mitzvoth* is captured in this observation by the English poet William Blake, in his epic poem *Jerusalem*: "He who would do good to another man must do it in Minute Particulars." The Bible might tell us to "love our neighbor," but the *mitzvoth* prescribe exact ways of doing this.

These "minute particulars" are typically divided in a variety of ways. Some treat the relationships between human beings. Others deal with the relationship between human beings and God, which I like to understand as the effort to strive toward godliness. The *mitzvoth* come in negative and positive forms. The negative *mitzvoth* range from prohibitions related to religious practice, such as not to work on *Rosh Hashanah*; to family, such as not to commit adultery or incest; to business ethics, such as not to commit fraud. The positive commandments tell us to rest on *Shabbat* or to honor your father and mother.

Even as a high percentage of the *mitzvoth* are strikingly modern, among the 613 biblical laws there are many that are archaic, irrelevant, and objectionable, which is inevitable given their antiquity. The rabbinic sages, who saw these laws as fixed, faced the dilemma in their own time of how to interpret commandments that they viewed as unacceptable, and addressed it through ingenious strategies of interpretation. For example, the Bible says that one should stone a rebellious son (Deuteronomy 21:18–21). The sages, without rejecting the biblical law directly, made implementing it impossible by subjecting it to absurd conditions. To be deemed "rebellious," the son had to be between the ages of thirteen and thirteen and three months; he had to steal a very precise amount of wine and meat; he had to be warned by his father and mother; and his parents had to have similar-sounding voices and be similar in appearance.

Today, as a Jew I feel free—even obliged—to question the relevance of many *mitzvoth* that are still commonly observed, such as the laws governing *kashrut*, the practice of keeping kosher. Though there are many theories about the origin of the dietary laws, I believe they were originally designed to separate the Jews from idol-worshipping pagans. But since we no longer live in pagan times, one can fairly ask if it makes sense to observe these prohibitions in all their detail. What I take from them as most useful is twofold: first, to be mindful of what we put in our bodies, and second, to do everything possible to reduce the suffering of animals slaughtered for food.

While it may be absurd to attempt to follow the 613 *mitzvoth* to the letter, it is even greater folly to simply reject the enormous fount of wisdom they offer. If we approach the 613 *mitzvoth* with the perspective of time and questioning minds, we find that they remain, even after thousands of years, a brilliant framework for carrying out Judaism's chief mission: to perfect and heal ourselves and our world. Rabbi Arnold Jacob Wolf, a leader of Reform Judaism who blended scholarship and a commitment to social justice, created an analogy for how to practice the *mitzvoth*. In his comments in *The Condition of Jewish Belief: A Symposium*, compiled by *Commentary* magazine in 1966, he compares Judaism to a road. Along the way the *mitzvoth* are buried like jewels. Some are too deeply in the ground to remove—those whose meaning is lost due to time, place, or circumstance. Others, such as lighting *Hanukkah* candles, are light and easy to pick up. Still others, like the ethical commandments, require greater strength and persistence to extricate.

Through practicing the *mitzvoth*, we can fulfill the sacred charge of Judaism: to pursue not just happiness, but justice. Generally speaking, the most important and relevant *mitzvoth* fit into one or more of these four overarching concepts:

Tzedakah
Hesed
Tikkun olam
Tikkun middot

In the sections below, I take on each of these concepts, first examining their place in Jewish tradition, then exploring how they have been brought to bear in the pursuit of justice by Jews today.

TZEDAKAH

Translated as "justice," not "charity," the concept of giving to others is absolutely central to the practice of Judaism. Writings on the concept of *tzedakah* examine not only its general principles but also the many shades of giving there can be. Maimonides describes the importance of giving cheerfully and with the receiver's welfare in mind:

One who gives *tzedakah* to a needy person with a sour expression, staring crossly at the floor, has lost and forfeited his merit. Rather, one should give *tzedakah* with a cheerful countenance, joyfully, and empathize with the other's troubles....If a needy person asks you for money and you have nothing to give him, [at least] encourage him verbally. It is forbidden to berate the needy person or to raise one's voice to him, for his heart is broken and melancholy....

Woe to one who humiliates a needy person—woe to him! Rather, one should act as a father to him. (Maimonides, Laws of Gifts to the Poor, 10:4–5)

Maimonides developed a ranking of levels of *tzedakah* that became known as Maimonides' ladder. Each rung on this ladder represents a different degree of virtue, beginning with the lowest form:

Giving begrudgingly.

Giving cheerfully but not in the right amount.

Giving cheerfully and in the right amount, but only after being asked.

Giving before being asked.

Giving so the donor doesn't know the receiver.

Giving so the receiver doesn't know the donor.

Giving so neither donor or receiver know each other's identities.

Giving money, time, a loan, or a business offer that enables the receiver to become self-reliant. (Laws of Gifts to the Poor, 10:7–14)

It is important to note that the lowest rung on the ladder, "Giving begrudgingly," is still a virtue. Even if you're doing something with the wrong intention, you're still on track. This is in keeping with Judaism's emphasis on making a practical difference in the world. Perhaps you have a friend in the hospital, but it's been an exhausting week and the last thing you want to do is sit at her bedside. But you go anyway. Judaism has no quarrel with this. In Judaism, we don't necessarily help others because we're especially loving or good people, but simply because it is the right thing to do. Of course it's always better to fulfill moral duties in a spirit of compassion, but it's not required.

Jewish law takes into account the difficulty of deciding when and how to give by mandating that we devote one-tenth of our income to the poor, which is the philosophy behind the practice of tithing. But in the end, however we choose to give, Judaism teaches that we must actively seek out opportunities, not wait for them to come our way. The prophets ceaselessly urge us to take care of the most vulnerable members of society—the widow, the orphan, and the stranger. "Justice, justice, shall you pursue," the Torah teaches (Deuteronomy 16:20). Regardless of how we feel, pursuing *tzedakah* is something we must seek and do.

Numerous studies find that Jews as a group are America's most generous and consistent donors, even when adjusting for income disparity. They have been the biggest contributors to causes that champion the oppressed, giving generously to gay, black, women's, and even, to the astonishment of many non-Jews, Palestinian organizations and charities. It is not a coincidence that since the New Deal, a majority of Jews have been Democrats, given that party's emphasis on structures that support society's most vulnerable members. Our tradition's commitment to redressing societal wrongs was a driving force behind the deep Jewish engagement in the civil rights movement. I am convinced that Judaism's imperative toward justice is the reason why Jews are disproportionately represented among social activists and those in fields that help others, in spite of the fact that many of these Jews are not religious in a traditional way.

HESED

Another type of giving in Judaism is *hesed*, a term that loosely translates as "loving-kindness" or "kind deeds." *Hesed*, like *tzedakah*, is a moral imperative: One must engage in it regardless of emotional inclination. But unlike *tzedakah*, which often refers to financial giving, *hesed* is usually associated with personal actions or deeds. For example, helping an elderly woman pick up her fallen groceries then carrying her bags home, even though she is headed in the opposite direction, would be considered an act of *hesed*.

The Talmud teaches that such everyday acts of *hesed* are absolutely essential to life. As we learn in the Talmudic book *Pirkei Avot*, or Ethics of the Fathers, the world is upheld on three pillars: the word of God (Torah); the worship of God (*avodah*); and the covenantal concept of loving-kindness (*hesed*). Our tradition calls on us to act from the highest, most morally developed part of our nature: "One is obligated to toil, exerting himself to the depths of his very soul, on behalf of his fellow man, be that person rich or poor. This is one of the most crucial and important things that men are called upon to do" (Rabbeinu Yonah, *The Gates of Repentance* 3:13).

TIKKUN OLAM

At its heart, Judaism, particularly Judaism in the twenty-first century, is a religion of *tikkun olam*—a term that is often translated as "repair of the world." There are many fascinating theories about the origin of today's usage of this term. According to tradition, it first showed up in the Mishnah, which is the earliest code of Jewish law and the basis for the Talmud. The term meant "to guard the established order." It has also been identified as part of a line in the Aleinu prayer, "*l'taken olam b'malchut shaddai*," which translates as "to make the world perfect under God's kingdom."

One of the most commonly identified roots of *tikkun olam* comes from a poetic parable attributed to Isaac Luria, a sixteenth-century rabbi who lived in the city of Safed in northern Israel. According to Luria, God placed parts of his own being into giant vessels. Overwhelmed by these loads of light, the vessels exploded and the brilliant sparks scattered throughout the universe. Eventually they became entrapped in matter. As the legend explains, practicing the commandments in the world liberates these primal sparks. When all are unleashed, the shattered vessels become whole. Through this parable, we come to understand that every moral or ethical action, no matter how small, contributes to making our world more perfect.

In another text related to the healing of the world, God tells Abraham to journey forth from the land of his birth. During his journey, Abraham sees a palace in flames. When God claims to own the palace, Abraham is aghast. Why would God allow the palace to be destroyed? God doesn't give much of an answer; he simply repeats that he is the owner of the palace (Genesis Rabbah 39:1). One possible reading is that the palace is a symbol for the world, and that human actions are destroying its magnificence. It is our responsibility, in our current understanding of *tikkun olam*, to put out the flames of hate, greed, poverty, and environmental destruction.

Whatever its origin, *tikkun olam* has became a rallying cry for Jews to uplift or repair the world. Many young Jews have taken this on as the central pillar of their practice of Judaism. When I began the Bronfman Youth Fellowships in Israel, a program that brings together young Jews from diverse backgrounds, I hoped that it would heal some of the rifts in the Jewish community and inspire Jews to more deeply engage in their tradition. As I have gotten to know year after year of Bronfman Fellows, I have been inspired by the emphasis on *tikkun olam* among them. Conversations with these young leaders, the oldest of whom are now in their forties, reveal the ways Jewish learning and community have inspired and informed their commitment to addressing injustice, both in the Jewish community and in the world at large.

One of these leaders is Jeremy Hockenstein, who founded an organization in Cambodia, Digital Divide Data, that puts into practice the highest rung of Maimonides' ladder of *tzeda-kah*: giving money, time, a loan, or a business offer that enables the receiver to become self-reliant. Digital Divide Data, as Jeremy described, "began when I traveled as a business consultant to Angkor Wat. I was struck by the mix of poverty and progress I saw in Cambodia. Though there were computer schools offering training to young people, there were still no jobs for the students once they graduated. I saw an opportunity to make a difference." Together with his friends Jason Rosenfeld, Kathryn Lucatelli, Scott Keller, Vernon Naidoo, and Shawn Fremeth, Jeremy decided to bring India's business process outsourcing model to Southeast Asia to provide jobs and contribute to the region's development. The company, which began as one small office in Phnom Penh, is now the largest technology-related employer in Cambodia and Laos. It has helped to develop a growing network of young professionals and propelled hundreds of families out of poverty. In a book of essays about the Bronfman Fellowships, Jeremy wrote that influence for this work came from many places, "but I know for sure that my participation in the Bronfman Fellowships program instilled in me the importance of seeking out work which makes a difference. It is particularly meaningful to me, as my mother was born in a concentration camp during the Holocaust, that now I am able to help another people rebuild from their genocide."

Taylor Krauss, another alumnus of the Bronfman Fellowships, speaks about how his Jewish identity helped inspire him to found Voices of Rwanda, an organization that collects the testimonies of survivors of the Rwandan genocide, during which over the course of ninety days in 1994 more than eight hundred thousand Tutsis were killed by their Hutu neighbors, without rescue from a passive international community. "For me," Taylor wrote, "'Never Again' means more than just keeping alive the terrible memory of the Holocaust. I feel it is a rallying cry to help prevent genocide and massacre wherever and whenever it is happening. Survival isn't just about acting in our own interest. As Jews—as human beings—we must not turn away from the suffering of others. As the sage Hillel asked, 'If I am not for myself, who will be for me? But if I am only for myself, who am I?'" Voices of Rwanda, as Taylor describes it, "recognizes the need of the rescapés [survivors] to share their stories and the value of their histories for all people. The testimonies will be made available as a resource for historians, psychologists, activists, journalists, artists, and future generations of Rwandans."

Like Jeremy and Taylor, I feel that Jews have a particular responsibility to guard against the horrors of genocide, and many have taken up the call. Most prominent in this effort is the American Jewish World Service, which has organized a broad Jewish communal response to the bloodshed in Darfur, a region in Sudan with a population of about 6 million that has undergone unbearable violence. When General Omar

Bashir took control of the Sudanese army by military coup, regional tensions were inflamed. In 2003, two Darfuri rebel movements fought against the Sudanese army. To cement its power, the Sudanese government sent in Arab militia known as Janjaweed, or "devils on horseback." The Janjaweed and the Sudanese army ravaged hundreds of defenseless villages throughout Darfur, destroying more than 400,000 lives and causing millions of civilians to flee. At present, according to UN figures, more than 2.7 million Darfuris are living in displaced persons camps and over 4.7 million depend on humanitarian aid for survival.

We say "Never Again" over and over, but this call cannot be limited to Jews. Nor can we ever be satisfied that we are doing enough, or turn our faces away. Older Jewish leaders should follow the example of younger Jews, for whom the urgency of alleviating suffering and fighting injustice has a profoundly Jewish resonance.

Hannah Rabinowitz, another Bronfman alumna, opened a thriving chapter of the national organization Challah for Hunger while she was a student at Yale University. Challah for Hunger raises money and awareness of social justice issues by bringing people together to bake and sell challah, the traditional Jewish bread. The project features chapters at campuses across the nation, each one baking and selling on average thirty to three hundred loaves of challah in a range of flavors, from chocolate to parsley-sage-rosemary-and-thyme. Every Challah for Hunger chapter donates half of its profits to a cause supported by a national organization. Other profits go to groups of each chapter's choosing. Hannah explained that "kneading 120 loaves worth of dough can be very time-consuming, let alone staying for another few hours to braid it into challah. But I truly believe in this. It is so rewarding for us to come together for a cause that is so essential, regardless of religious or social background."

Another alumna of the Bronfman Fellowships whose work makes me particularly proud is Idit Klein, who founded Keshet, a group that promotes equality for the LGBT community in the Jewish world. In my many conversations with Idit, I've come to understand the Jewish dimension of the struggle for LGBT rights, an issue that has concerned me for many years. In the early 1970s, while I was CEO of the Seagram Company, public dialogue about gay rights was largely nonexistent in corporate America. Social discourse had not yet even evolved into the "don't ask, don't tell" ethos that dominated the following decades. Homosexuality was simply not discussed, and therefore, by implication, was shameful. During that time, since I was the head of a company with thousands of employees, personnel issues often came across my desk.

One day the director of human resources came into my office with a recommendation to terminate one of my brightest executives. I found myself puzzled that anyone would want to fire such a promising young man until the director leaned in and confided in a hushed tone, "Well, you know, he's a homosexual."

The declaration did persuade me—but not in the way he had hoped. The promising young executive continued on to a distinguished career at Seagram, and the HR director was soon let go. Although my choice was shocking to the director, the decision was obvious to me: To fire a person because of his sexual orientation was not only wrong, it was bad business. It was discrimination, plain and simple, and would not be tolerated in the company I ran.

My response that day was entirely instinctive: To deny individuals anything because of sexual orientation makes no sense. Anyone who would feel otherwise is someone whose intellectual acumen I would not trust. Over forty years later, I feel that the same common sense applies to the issue of marriage equality. It is just plain wrong to take roughly 10 percent of the population in this country and tell them that they are second-class citizens, denying them the basic civil rights, such as medical, tax, and family benefits, that are protected in heterosexual marriages. Without question, the recent Supreme Court ruling on this issue was an act of *tikkun olam.*

It has been a privilege and joy, in my work with initiatives to engage Jewish young people, to know so many who are dedicating themselves to healing our broken world. I am inspired by the work being done at the Bronfman Center at New York University to foster dialogue between young Muslims and Jews that is based on respect and understanding. Currently, a rabbi and an imam co-teach a course entitled "Multifaith

Leadership in the Twenty-First Century." A group called "Bridges: Muslim-Jewish Dialogue" leads community service trips to disaster zones, working together to provide humanitarian relief to people who are suffering. The interfaith cooperation extends into the student dorms, where Jewish and Muslim students dedicated an entire floor of the residence as a place to live and study together. Their effort toward being models of mutual respect is a marvelous example of *tikkun olam*.

TIKKUN MIDDOT

As *tikkun olam* addresses the repair of the outer world, the less well-known concept of *tikkun middot* addresses repair of our inner world. In Hebrew, *middot* literally means "measures," as in the weights on a scale, but it has the secondary meaning of character attributes such as generosity, humbleness, and the ability to forgive.

Engaging in the hard work of identifying and admitting where we have erred is a real challenge. For years my leadership positions in both the business world and in Jewish political circles have made me face criticism, warranted and unwarranted, and I have committed offenses, both intentional and unintentional, and had them committed against me. Such inconsistencies are the nature of relationships, both personal and professional, and we all navigate them as best we can.

But Judaism requires us to do more than navigate. It requires us to consistently take stock and to repair ourselves when our moral tank is running on empty. This responsibility is evident in the Hebrew word for prayer—*tefilah*—which means to judge oneself. In Judaism, self-improvement can be thought of as a kind of prayer.

My own practice of *tikkun middot* involves an action I've dubbed the mirror test. At least once a week, I gaze at my reflection and decide whether or not I'm happy with the man looking back. If not, why not? Have I hurt someone or made a mistake? Where have I failed myself or others? What positive attributes do I need to strengthen? What negative traits do I need to address? Where am I out of balance? Of course, real change requires more than looking in a mirror and asking oneself questions. But this kind of self-examination is a start.

In sum, Judaism is not concerned with saving souls for heaven, but with saving lives on earth. In Judaism, abortion is not murder; evolution is not blasphemy; stem-cell research is not apostasy. The history of Judaism is that secular science and sacred values are allies. Salvation is not secured by dogma but by moral wisdom. Through the enactment of the *mitzvoth*, through the practice of *tikkun olam* and *tikkun middot*, we can immerse ourselves in the Jewish mission: to do, to create, and to accomplish those things that make a better society for all.

But it would be a mistake to think that "doing" is only represented by action in the world. Just as important to Judaism is studying. With that, we turn to the importance of text study, something which I believe should be at the center of our Jewish practice.

Part II

CHAPTER 4

The Tree and the Sea

One who is shy will not learn.

—Hillel, *Pirkei Avot* 2:6

Just as rain water comes down in drops and forms rivers, so with the Torah; one studies a bit today and some more tomorrow, until in time it becomes like a flowing stream.

—Song of Songs Rabbah

The highest activity a human being can attain is learning for understanding, because to understand is to be free.

—Baruch Spinoza, *Ethics*

JEWS ARE OFTEN REFERRED TO AS "PEOPLE OF THE Book." In the Quran, this term describes non-Muslim adherents to monotheistic faiths and includes both Jews and Christians. In Jewish parlance it refers to the idea that regardless of the numerous countries we have inhabited throughout our history, we have held on to certain textual traditions—our Torah and Talmud—with greater certainty than any geographical terrain.

The phrase can also be seen as encompassing the overall value Judaism places on learning, including the study of secular subjects. Intellectual achievement has been a hallmark of Jews for generations. Throughout its history, Judaism has placed enormous emphasis on teaching its young and cultivating the acquisition of knowledge among a broad (though until more recent years, largely male) portion of its population. In fact, as one of my teachers, former Columbia University chaplain Rabbi Michael Paley, points out in an interview in the journal *Kerem*, "We refer to our greatest Biblical leader not as Moshe HaNavi (Moses, our prophet) or Moshe Malkeinu (our leader or king), but as Moshe Rabbeinu—our teacher."

This emphasis on education started very early in the tradition and always stayed front and center. Maimonides believed so passionately in the importance of education that he declared the teaching of children to be the responsibility of all Jews. If a town refused to hire a teacher, he wrote, then that town should be excommunicated. If that wasn't enough to convince its people, the town should be destroyed (Maimonides, Laws of Talmud Torah, 2:1). This is a harsh approach, even for today, but even more so when you consider the time in which Maimonides lived.

It might seem strange to us now in this era of compulsory education, but attending school was once a rare privilege. During the Talmudic period, it is notable that formal schooling for every Jewish boy began at the age of six. The Talmud's many volumes of wisdom were never intended to be just for scholars or rabbis (though it has taken much time and effort for women to work toward full inclusion in traditions of Jewish study).

In my own family, my struggling grandfather, Ekiel Bronfman, brought a *melamed*, a teacher, for his young family when he left what is now Moldova for a small town in Saskatchewan, Canada. I never met my grandfather—he died of stomach cancer in 1924, five years before I was born—but I was always struck by his decision to bring both seeds and a teacher to the new world. Nurturing his children's minds was clearly as important to him as putting food on the table.

Today, one can see the fruits of the Jewish emphasis on education in the remarkable levels of learning and scholarship among Jews in many fields. As I have said previously, I believe that it is a fundamentally Jewish practice to study and strive for excellence in the humanities and other secular fields. But it is striking that absent from the bookshelves of many highly educated Jews today are the foundational texts of the Jewish people: the Torah and the Talmud. On the shelves of spiritual seekers, Jewish and otherwise, you are far more likely to encounter English translations of the Bhagavad Gita, the Dhammapada, the Analects of Confucius, and other Eastern classics than volumes of the Talmud and Torah.

This absence may be due in part to the bad rap these books have received. Many intelligent people consider the Torah a dusty compendium of ancient genealogies. The Talmud has fared even worse, cast as a formidable and antiquated compilation of mental jigsaw puzzles, bizarre stories, hairsplitting arguments, and mind-numbing legalistic discourse written in an archaic language for pious, bearded men. To borrow Winston Churchill's famous line about Russia, I think many would define the Talmud as "a riddle wrapped in a mystery inside an enigma."

But in my own journey I have found that this could not be further from the truth. The Torah and Talmud, arguably the oldest living books still in continual use, record the stories, beliefs, and commentary that make up our tradition. Though they are often presented as books of faith, as a nontheistic Jew, I see them as a vast collection of wisdom, a vibrant connection to my heritage, and a means of understanding the world through a Jewish lens. Through their study and discussion, I have discovered many practical insights on how to live an honorable life dedicated to creating harmony between people and within myself.

The sections that follow aim to provide a very basic understanding of the place of the Torah and the Talmud in the Jewish tradition and to help modern Jews make their own connections to the books that are known, respectively, as "the tree" and "the sea."

THE TORAH

The Torah is so central to Jewish tradition that religious Jews refer to it as the Tree of Life, for like a tree it nourishes, protects, and sustains. From ancient times to within today's Orthodox streams of Judaism, many have considered the Torah to be divinely written. However, most scholars and liberal Jews agree that it is a collection of oral stories that were told over a span of time, written down by many redactors, and possibly codified (though the jury is still out on this) by a super-editor called Ezra the Scribe.

The written Torah, a word that translates as "the Teaching," is the foundational book of the Jewish people. In its most common usage, "the Torah" refers to the Five Books of Moses: Genesis, Exodus, Leviticus, Numbers, and Deuteronomy. These books, which are the text of the Torah scrolls read in synagogue, form one of the three parts of the Hebrew Bible. The other two parts are Prophets (Judges, Samuel, Kings, Isaiah, Jeremiah, Ezekiel, and the Twelve Later Prophets) and Writings (David's Psalms, Solomon's Proverbs, the Five Megillot, or Scrolls, the books of Ezra and Nehemiah, and Chronicles). Together, this collection is generally referred to as the Old Testament by Christians, who believe that these writings were superseded by the New Testament.

After the sacking of the Second Temple in Jerusalem by the Romans in 70 CE, exiled Jews joined existing Jewish communities elsewhere or formed new ones throughout the world. Over the next hundreds of years, the Torah became a kind of portable Temple, something that the Jewish people could access wherever they wandered. The Torah is a collection of writings, but its depth and meaning are also contained in its interplay with its readers over many years, from the interpretations of the biblical prophets through the commentaries of medieval sages and modern scholars. Our sages say the Torah is so rich that each verse has seventy facets or faces, a visual image suggesting that many interpretations are possible.

Several rabbinic commentaries liken the Torah to "black fire on white fire." The black fire is the letters and the white the space between. In some interpretations of this fascinating image, the rabbis suggest that while the text must remain true to its literal meaning, the white fire represents everything that goes beyond the fixed meaning. To my mind, this poetic and powerful image captures the live and luminous quality of Jewish law and teachings.

Told in prose embedded with startling imagery, and including poetry that at times reaches an incandescent pitch, the stories of the Torah, when viewed as literature and allegory, contain piercing psychological and spiritual insights that can be as relevant today as they were thousands of years ago. With stories ranging from the creation of the universe to the death of Moses, the Torah contains every sort of character: the valorous and the vindictive, the good and the greedy, the morally fine and the seriously flawed. With all their contradictions, the stories in the Torah, like all great literature, are a trove of timeless wisdom.

In my study of the Torah I have found much that is meaningful and thought-provoking. I have always been particularly fascinated by Moses. Whether he is a fictional character or a historical figure is irrelevant to the power and complexity he possesses as the protagonist of Exodus, the Jewish people's most enduringly resonant story. Moses is not a cardboard hero. He is a human being who is both brave and timid, who is capable of great feats and just as many failures. More than anything, he is the embodiment of a leader, which I will discuss in more detail in a later chapter. My study of Moses inspired me in my work as head of the World Jewish Congress: Through him, I learned the skills, strategies, and attitudes needed to effectively lead. I also came to understand that a leader must be rebellious, because unless you have the ability to challenge the status quo you won't be able to envision a new future, much less lead people toward it in spite of their fears and doubts.

Moses' story also taught me that when confronting overwhelming challenges, it is critical to fight the natural desire to remain cautious and scale back on the dream. Above all he taught me that a leader must have deep sensitivity to the wants and needs of those being led, even when it might be exasperating to listen. In fact, the story of Moses gave me the courage to write this book, no small feat at the age of eighty-four and a half.

THE TALMUD

Without the definite article, "Torah" can refer to the whole corpus of Jewish law and teachings. The Oral Torah expanded on the meaning of biblical stories and concepts, and these orally spoken ideas, coming from dozens of rabbinic sages over several centuries, were eventually compiled into a written document known as the Mishnah. Over time, the Mishnayot (plural of Mishnah) were further elaborated upon, and these embroideries became known as the Gemara, an ancient Aramaic word meaning "to finish." Originally separate, the Mishnah and Gemara were ultimately synthesized into a fascinating series of books known as the Talmud.

The Talmud has been referred to as "the sea." Like the sea, its pages are full of currents and crosscurrents; they virtually teem with life. The Talmud, in fact, is so deep that people can devote their entire lives to their study and barely get below the surface. Albert Einstein recognized this when he sent a statement to Professor Chaim Tchernowitz in praise of the scholar's work in making the Talmud accessible to a wider readership. He wrote:

The scientific organization and comprehensive exposition in accessible form of the Talmud has a twofold importance for us Jews. It is important in the first place that the high cultural values of the Talmud should not be lost to modern minds among the Jewish people nor to science, but should operate further as a living force.

During the earliest stage of the Talmud's development, conversations and discourses that interpreted the Torah were memorized and recited aloud by sages known as *tannaim*, or "repeaters." As they recited, the *tannaim* interspersed their own commentary, embroidering on the meaning. Many reasons might account for this oral system of transmission, one of them being that, like the holy Temple itself, written books could be burned. Another reason for oral teaching was that the rabbis understood the Bible to prohibit committing the Oral Torah to writing. The spoken nature of the Oral Torah allowed for more give-and-take in teaching and greater flexibility in establishing religious law that addressed the changing needs of the Jewish people.

The rabbis of the Talmud recognized that great truths are embedded in the Torah's stories and declarations, but constantly challenged and updated the meaning of its laws and ideas. For example, the sages wrestled with the meaning of the biblical phrase "eye for eye, tooth for tooth" (Exodus 21:24). A literal reading would see this as a clear call for vengeful retribution. However, the sages, in a series of discussions, interpreted this line to mean a payment in proportion to the injury, not physical retaliation.

It is also fascinating to see what the sages make of the

Torah's commandment that we "honor our mother and father." The rabbis take on the questions that arise when we confront what it means to put this commandment into practice: What are our emotional, financial, and care obligations toward our parents? Whom do we honor in a quarrel? If we have to choose between supporting our parents and providing for our spouse or children, what do we do? And what does "honor" really mean anyway? Blind obedience? Refraining from insult? Not sitting in a parent's chair? Not challenging? How far does our obligation extend? Always concerned with the practical action, rabbinic law and legend, along with our tradition's medieval and modern ethical tracts, provide very specific guidelines for ways this commandment should be translated into concrete actions and prohibitions.

I grappled with the meaning of this very difficult commandment after the death of my own father, Samuel Bronfman, with whom my relationship was troubled and contentious. When I decided to start a vehicle through which I could make charitable contributions, I knew I needed to name the organization The Samuel Bronfman Foundation. In founding Seagram, my father had built a great company and done a great deal of good for the Canadian Jewish community, and I felt I should publicly recognize this. But given our past history it wasn't so easy to do.

The emphasis our sages place on honoring our parents helped me through this difficulty. I remember several Talmudic teachings in particular. In one, we are taught that if a father throws his wallet into the sea, the son should not rebuke him for it. His silence is a form of honor (Kiddushin 32a). In similar spirit, another sage describes a son who had an elderly mother whom he treated with such respect that whenever she wanted to get into bed he would bend down and she would climb on him. When she descended from the bed, she would step on him to reach the floor (Kiddushin 31b). These are extreme examples, but they are not untypical, and, generally speaking, when we encounter such exaggeration in the Talmud, it is for the purpose of driving home a point.

The rabbis, however, were not unrealistic, and their strong assertions about filial piety are often balanced by more moderate views. For example, in the case of the wallet, they opined that if it is the son's wallet, he can later sue the father in court to recover the money, and in the Hebrew Bible we learn, "For your own sake, therefore, be most careful," which could mean that our own well-being is an important factor to consider when fulfilling the prescribed duties of filial piety (Deuteronomy 4:15). Maimonides also notes that "if the mind of his father or his mother is affected, the son should make every effort to indulge the vagaries of the stricken parent until God will have mercy on the afflicted. But if the condition of the parent has grown worse, and the son is no longer able to endure the strain, he may leave his father or mother, go elsewhere, and delegate others to give the parent proper care" (Maimonides, Laws of Apostasy, 6:10).

Along with in-depth legal discussions that take place across generations, the Talmud interprets the Torah through a type of story known as a *midrash*. Central to the idea of *midrash*, a word that means "investigation" or "inquiry," is that the Bible contains many gaps and that it must be read in between the lines. A *midrash* is a story or commentary that fills in the parts of the Bible that seem unclear or incomplete. In many cases, *midrashim* (plural of *midrash*) add dialogue and detail to the lives of biblical characters. The tradition of *midrash* leads the way to constant reinterpretation, steering us away from fundamentalism or strictly literal reading.

One of my favorite *midrashim* involves Moses' use of advanced psychology to assuage a flock of unhappy angels. When they learn God is giving the Torah to Moses, the angels are very annoyed and say to God, "Do you intend to squander this precious commodity on mankind?" God commands Moses to answer, and Moses gives an indirect response. "The Torah," he explains, "expressly forbids idolatry, murder, adultery, and theft. Are angels even capable of such behavior? Do you need to be told not to murder or steal or bear false witness or to honor your parents? You are far too developed to do such wrongdoings." The angels concede (Shabbat 88B–89A).

What a brilliant answer! To disagree with Moses' explanation, the angels would have to refute their own exalted status. But there is another way to read this enigmatic little story. As I see it, the *midrash* plainly underscores an idea put forth in Deuteronomy that the Torah was not created for perfect beings in heavens, but for the less perfect people of earth. Judaism is

all about attaining the sacred in the human world through fulfilling the moral obligations of the *mitzvoth*: This is our route to
holiness.

The Talmud offers a road map to a grounded spirituality
that encompasses both human relationships and the natural world. Among its laws are instructions to give thanks for
natural fragrances and for the perfumes derived from them:
We are commanded to thank God when we catch the aroma
of roses, myrtle, rosemary, jasmine, citrus blossom, mint,
hyacinth, and honeysuckle, as well as cloves, cinnamon, and
ground coffee. As a nonreligious Jew, I turn my gratitude to
the source of the fragrances themselves—the flowers, the
fruits, and the spices that fill our world with pleasure.

The topics in the Talmud range from the mundane to
the mystical. When read searchingly, these astonishing texts
uncover nothing less than the mysteries of human nature and
the universe. Like great jazz musicians, the sages riff on innu-
merable themes and ideas with an intellectual inventiveness
and verbal acrobatics that can be breathtakingly beautiful or
marvelously humorous. While many individual commentaries will sound off-key or discordant to contemporary ears, as
a whole they invite us to mull over meaning, encourage us to
ask hard questions, and encourage us to logically engage our
minds and push the envelope of interpretation.

While study of Talmud has long been limited mostly to the
Orthodox world, in recent years it has been taken up by liberal Jews. One who is leading the charge in Israel is Dr. Ruth

Calderon, a newly elected member of the Israeli Knesset and founder of Elul and Alma, two secular houses of Talmudic study that include women. In May 2013, in her first speech to the Knesset, she makes the point that though political expediency required leaders to hand over too much control of aspects of Jewish life to religiously oriented groups, she believes—and I agree—that it is time to take that back. In her speech she encapsulates what I've been thrilled to hear throughout our many conversations:

> It is impossible to stride toward the future without knowing where we came from and who we are, without knowing, intimately and in every particular, the sublime as well as the outrageous and the ridiculous. The Torah is not the property of one movement or another. It is a gift that every one of us received, and we have all been granted the opportunity to meditate upon it as we create the realities of our lives. Nobody took the Talmud and rabbinic literature from us. We gave it away, with our own hands, when it seemed that another task was more important and urgent: building a state, raising an army, developing agriculture and industry, etc. The time has come to re-appropriate what is ours, to delight in the cultural riches that wait for us, for our eyes, our imaginations, our creativity.

In one of my discussions with Dr. Calderon, she described the rapture she felt during her first encounter with the

Talmud: "When I first seriously opened a page of Talmud, I was amazed. I was in love. I wasn't touching the ground for a whole year. I was floating. And the book is so surprising. So rich, so funny, so wild, so clever. It's much more than a book. It's a world."

I'm delighted that tens of thousands of Jews across the world are taking part in the Talmud-reading project known as Daf Yomi, a Hebrew phrase meaning "page of the day" or "daily folio," which began in 1923 in Vienna. The project has taken on new life with the English-language publication of seventy-two volumes of the Babylonian Talmud by ArtScroll. While Daf Yomi was originally designed as a way for religious Jews to connect, it is now being enthusiastically embraced by increasing numbers of secular Jews. One of these is Adam Kirsch, a literary critic and contributing editor to *Tablet*, an online Jewish magazine. In the form of brief, highly readable essays, Adam has been chronicling his experience with Daf Yomi, bringing the Talmud's "enchantments and difficulties, its law and logic and legends, the questions and answers and counter-questions it provokes." His essays, written in a plain and easy style, make a great entry point to the Talmud.

Newcomers to study of both the Torah and Talmud are also embracing a classic Jewish method known as *hevruta*, an Aramaic term meaning "fellowship." In this age-old method of study, two students work in tandem, exploring a text together, talking out loud, and volleying ideas back and forth. In lively dialogue, they explore contradictory statements, examine the shades of meaning in individual words, and attempt to tie together things that otherwise seem disconnected. Rabbis and teachers grapple with the issues alongside their students. Opinions are explored, opposite ideas entertained. And while not all interpretations are right, and there are rules of engagement, the playing field is very wide.

This communal model of Talmudic learning creates a democratic culture that values multiple opinions and doesn't take kindly to dogma. The Jewish enterprise involves a rigorous search for answers to questions big and small, but also recognizes that fixed meaning is elusive: Meaning shifts according to the observer and is subject to multiple interpretations. According to the Bible, King Solomon wrote three thousand parables to draw out the meaning of each biblical verse.

Some of my most fulfilling—and noisy—Jewish moments have been around the study of texts, a practice for which I have made space in my everyday life. Every week, I convene a study group made up of several study partners and a leader: a Jewish thinker, teacher, or rabbi. In my work with Hillel and the Bronfman Fellowships, I have had the opportunity to sit in *hevruta* with high school students, college students, and young leaders. And I have studied with my grandchildren, whose questions and insights, even at a very young age, add challenge and enrichment.

From the first stories of Genesis, our texts raise questions that can be taken on by inquiring minds of all ages and backgrounds. Take, for example, the story of Adam and Eve in the Garden of Eden. Eve, as the well-known story goes, is tricked by a serpent into taking a bite of the forbidden fruit from the Tree of Knowledge. In turn, she causes Adam to eat the forbidden fruit, and both are cast out to the fate we all know: Toil will be their lot; bread will be earned by the sweat of their brow.

For me, the text brings up a basic question: If God hadn't wanted human beings to eat of the Tree of Knowledge, why was it planted there in the first place? What was he thinking? What's wrong with him? To take this approach within the Jewish tradition is not regarded as sacrilege. There are no fences around the mind.

Because the Torah does not reveal inner lives as much as narrate events, the tradition of *midrash* encourages us to make them our own by speculating on the psychology and emotional states of the characters. Consider the story of Cain and Abel. These two young men, the sons of Adam and Eve, are engaged in a feud so bitter that out of jealousy Cain murders his own brother. When God confronts him for his dastardly act, Cain challenges him. The biblical story stops there. But rabbinical expansion—an expansion you can do too—adds dialogue: Cain says to God, "Why do you ask me where Abel is? You know where everything is. And how was I supposed to know that if I hit him on the head with a rock he would die? You put my rage and my resentment inside of me, so it's your fault. And if you hadn't preferred his offering over mine, this would not have happened in the first place. The murder of Abel is your fault!"

For one who is studying text, this added dialogue can quickly expand into a discussion of free will and human responsibility, the subtleties of right and wrong. It also encourages us to attempt to explain the Bible's many inconsistencies, a kind of creative interaction that allows us to deeply integrate our own selves into the stories.

Studying is a wonderful way to bring generations together. I remember one session at Harvard Hillel when I sat down with a redheaded student easily thirty years my junior. The passage assigned to the room was the one where Aaron makes a golden calf for the Israelites to worship at Mount Sinai. We were asked to explain what was happening. We dove into the text and finally decided that Aaron was trying to quell a rebellion brewing in the ranks through the making of a bull, something that had been part of the law-and-order system of the Egyptians. It was a wonderful process, and as we lobbed ideas back and forth, the age and distance between us quickly faded away.

Communal study of Talmud and Torah teaches us that true learning comes when we seriously converse with those different from ourselves. This is a very worthwhile attitude to cultivate, especially given today's tendency to socialize with groups who mirror our own political and cultural beliefs. We tend to find our camps and stick to them—for example, liberal on one side, conservative to the other. Such a closed-minded attitude does no one any favors.

Text study also has the power to fulfill the individual seeker. Some years ago, my son Adam, who is now managing director of The Samuel Bronfman Foundation, shared with me that he could do self-exploration better when discussing Torah and Talmud than when left to his own devices. Many scholars have even gone further, noting that study of these rich texts has been a profoundly spiritual experience.

Another benefit to text study? Its critical method sharpens the intellect. There has been a trend in Korea and China to undertake the study of Talmud to prepare the mind for success in business. I understand there is even a Talmud hotel in Taiwan that features the "Talmud Business Success Bible" on the bedside table. As happy as I am when the world's people admire the Jews and see value in Jewish study, this is an example of misguided thinking. These great books do not offer secret codes to wealth and success, but a wisdom that explores, with argumentation, humor, stories, and endless commentary, how to bring sparks of moral and ethical light into the world.

The Talmud features two ancient sages: Hillel, who was considered tolerant and kind, and Shammai, who was thought to be strict and unbending in his interpretations of the law. In one of the Hillel and Shammai stories, a non-Jew approaches them and asks to be taught the whole of the Torah while standing on one leg. Infuriated by the disrespectful, mocking request, Shammai strikes him with a measuring rod, whereas Hillel replies, "That which is hateful to you, do not do unto another. That is the whole Torah. The rest is commentary— [and now] go study" (Shabbat 31a).

Today, the line "the rest is commentary" is often interpreted as something nonessential or beside the point. That is not what Hillel meant to express. The central charge of the Torah is to be kind and loving to our fellow beings. But to really understand that message, to enact it in the fullest way possible, Hillel recommends that we study the wisdom—the commentary—found in the sacred books.

It is never too late to begin this process. One of the greatest Jewish sages, Rabbi Akiva, did not begin to learn until he was forty years old. Legend has it that Akiva was standing by a well, witnessing how the water had shaped the rock, and asked himself if his mind had become more rigid than stone. Where, he wondered, was the source of water that could help shape him? He resolved at that moment to study Judaism and took himself with all due humility to sit in a child's classroom and begin to learn as a novice. He approached learning with modesty and curiosity, and it is said he studied for forty years and went on to become one of the greatest thinkers to shape Jewish learning for millennia (Avot d'Rabbi Natan 6:2).

From these stories, and so many like them, we learn that study is central to the history and practice of Judaism. For many years, it has held our people together as communities and families. In the next chapter, I turn to that idea of family, another concept at the heart of the Jewish tradition.

CHAPTER 5

The Little Sanctuary

One who teaches his son Torah, it is considered as if he taught his son, his son's son, and so on to the end of generations.

—Talmud, Kiddushin 30a

Honor your father and mother.

—Exodus 20:12; Deuteronomy 5:16

ONE OF THE THINGS I TREASURE MOST ABOUT Judaism is its emphatic insistence on the importance of family. We constantly find the message that life should be led within the community's embrace, not in isolation, and that family is at the center of that community. My own home growing up was quite formal—I mostly feared my father, and my mother was often remote—but the Jewish emphasis on family was nonetheless a sacrosanct value.

This value resonated with me during one of the most

moving moments in my life: when I received a last blessing from my maternal grandfather. Throughout my childhood Gramps and I had been very close. He was tall, with a goatee, and though religious, he was not overly serious. He had a carefree manner and was always advising everyone to "take it easy." This attitude came through in everything about him. On the eve of my sister's wedding, for example, an uncle died. As an educated, religious Jew, Gramps was asked to rule on whether or not the wedding should go forward. Consistent with his character, he ruled in favor of the *mitzvah* that said joy should overcome sadness.

I also remember how Gramps would take me, my brother, and our cousins to a tiny hole-in-the-wall deli called Ben's and on mountain walks. As we noshed on smoked meat sandwiches or strolled through the crisp air, Gramps would quietly share his experiences with us, easily moving from the personal to the philosophical. But whatever the topic, he never instructed. He just talked and gave us the space to arrive at our own conclusions.

When I was in my early twenties, I went to see him. I somehow sensed that this would be the last time we would meet (and it was), so I asked him for a blessing. I can still see him wrapping himself up in his blue-and-white prayer shawl, striking a match, and lighting a candle. As he recited the ancient words, I felt moved to my marrow. I could almost physically feel an invisible thread joining us—first me to him, and then the two of us to our ancient forebears. With this, I stepped into a cycle of existence far greater than anything I could ever know or hope to understand, something I found immensely reassuring. To this day, whenever I recall the sensation of his hand gently resting on my head and hear the musical sound of his soft Hebrew in my memory, I am overwhelmed by an indescribable sense of loss and longing.

Sadly, the bond I felt then to my Jewish heritage did not further develop, and shortly thereafter I abandoned it altogether. Part of this, I'm sure, is that despite my closeness to my grandfather, my connection to Judaism was weak. My parents, for whatever reason, failed to instill much-needed Jewish pride in their children. Though they gave us some Jewish education and contributed generously to Jewish causes during the war, my father seemed extremely conflicted about his Judaism; I would go so far as to say that he harbored animosity. The contradictory ways in which the Judaism of my parents expressed itself created a deep ambivalence in me. One area in which this ambivalence played itself out was their choices for my education.

Because Father was a real Anglophile—he loved everything English—my brother, Charles, and I did not attend Jewish schools, but were sent to the Selwyn House School, a place that enrolled few Jewish boys. This arrangement resulted in our having two sets of friends: the Protestants at Selwyn House, and the Jewish kids from the synagogue, a place we viewed with less than enthusiasm. I don't think my parents ever understood how confusing this arrangement was for their children and how in my eyes it automatically reduced our

Jewish friends to the status of second-class companions. Even now, decades later, I am not clear on why I thought less of my Jewish friends than of my elite Protestant companions. I am afraid it's because I was reflecting my parents' feelings on the subject.

My parents' ambivalence about their Jewishness also showed up when I procured a golf caddy job at the Alpine Inn. There was a man from New York, a Mr. Kenny, who insisted on an English-speaking caddy. Unless he had one, he would take his business elsewhere. As English-speaking caddies were rare, I sensed a negotiating opportunity and in the end not only got the caddying job but succeeded in getting to play golf for free in the afternoon.

When I arrived home, I proudly told Mother of my employment victory. When she heard my story, her face took on a worried expression, and she informed me that I wasn't strong enough to caddy. Since my mother wasn't a typical Jewish mother, this response struck me as unusual. But when I hotly contested her assessment of my abilities, she offered no explanation. Instead, she offered to pay me what I would make in the morning if I agreed not to caddy in the afternoon.

What I didn't know at the time was that the Alpine Inn was restricted—Jews were not welcome. Rather than tackle the topic of anti-Semitism head-on, Mother avoided it. In fact, she bought me off. In the end, this was all very confusing to a fifteen-year-old boy.

The Judaism of my parents and of my own generation was

not a joyful Judaism. It was one forged in the fires of pogroms in Russia from which my grandparents fled, and deepened by the horror of the Holocaust. Although we were safe in Canada, the pain of the millions of Jews being murdered in Europe rested heavily on our shoulders. There was a vague, haunting sadness to being a Jewish child in the 1940s, even in the relative safety of North America. The calamity happening overseas was never discussed in our home, but we all knew anyway. Anti-Semitism during my youth, albeit less dramatic than the evils in Europe, was nonetheless damaging to the Jewish psyche. It wasn't just the physical manifestations of anti-Semitism: It was also an injury to the sense of self.

Despite their immense wealth, my parents did not escape this pain. On the one hand they were clearly Jews, but on the other they were empire builders who longed to be bona fide members of the non-Jewish power elite, the majority of whom were not welcoming of Jews. Though they never said so, my guess is that if others had allowed them to do so, they might have cast off their Jewish identity at the first opportunity.

My lack of pride in my Jewishness might explain why I didn't protest my first wife's custom of celebrating Christmas, something not unusual for highly assimilated German Jews of that generation. I am sure that if I had voiced opposition Ann would have given up the holiday and would also have agreed to give the children as much Jewish education as I wanted. But I didn't object because it wasn't important to me. So for many years we hung stockings by our fireplace and set up our fir tree, a grand and glittering affair that made no pretense at masquerading as that odd American invention, the *Hanukkah* bush. On Christmas morning the air would fill with the excited squeals of our five children as they emptied their stockings and tore open their presents. I was not completely comfortable with all of this, especially receiving gifts from my in-laws, Petey and John Loeb, but since I lacked any real connection to my Jewishness, I dismissed my feelings as unimportant.

Looking back, I believe that had my parents consciously instilled Jewish pride in me during my formative years, I would not have been so woefully indifferent to my Judaism. But I can't really blame them, because I followed in their footsteps and failed to give my own children even the very basic Jewish education I'd received. If there is anything I regret, it is that as my children grew up, I gave them no Jewish tradition in our home. There was no Friday night meal to welcome the *Shabbat*, no observance of the holidays, and no Jewish learning.

This failing still haunts me. It is one of the reasons I spearheaded the Bronfman Youth Fellowships in Israel, a training program for young leaders. It's also why I have thrown myself and my resources into the revival of Hillel houses on campus and into the creation of MyJewishLearning.com, a website that offers information about Judaism from the most basic questions to advanced study and inquiry. And it's why I am so thrilled when Bronfman Fellowships alumni, like Rabbi Daniel Smokler, who is now director of education at the

Bronfman Center at New York University, commit to bringing Jewish learning and text study to other young people in a way that is joyful and personal.

Still, while initiatives and programs are much needed, love of Judaism begins with family, at home. After the destruction of the Second Temple in 70 CE, our sages determined that the home would become the new Temple, calling it a *mikdash ma'at*, or little sanctuary. As one *midrash* explains, "When the Temple stood, the altar offered atonement for Israel. Now, one's table offers atonement" (Brachot 55a). The Jewish home—or any home—should be more than a shelter: It should act as the center of meaning, beauty, and connection to forces larger than ourselves.

In Jewish tradition, it is in the home that many of life's significant milestones, from the birth of a child to death and mourning, take place. As pointed out by Rabbi Andy Bachman, a well-known communal leader and dear friend, Judaism has rituals for all those aspects of life—birth, transition, marriage, death—in which people cry out for meaning. He believes, and I think I agree, that these life-sanctifying rituals, along with *Shabbat*, are one of the main reasons that Judaism has stayed alive for nearly four thousand years.

The marking of these ancient customs brings joy and comfort into our present lives and joins us to our past. Below is a brief sampling of some of the key events in the Jewish life cycle, along with suggestions for how they can be practiced by those with nonreligious orientations. I share my ideas and experience with the aim of helping others to make the joy and wisdom of Judaism a blessing between their family members and within their homes.

BABY NAMING

Baby-naming traditions have always fascinated me. In the United Kingdom, traditional names rule the roost, and the royal family is a source of much inspiration. Chinese baby naming is fairly complicated, as parents consider the number of brushstrokes that form the name to ensure a balance of male and female energies, or yin and yang. Catholics focus on biblical names, and boys often get the names of fathers and grandfathers. Parents in India often look to the stars, while African baby names often reflect parental aspirations for the newborn child. Not surprisingly, the name Barack, which comes from the Arabic root for "blessings" (which is close to the Hebrew word for blessing, *beracha*), was generally used only in East Africa, but since the election of Barack Obama has gained traction all over the continent. Muslim cultures often focus on names that honor the Prophet, which is why in Arab and Islamic countries you will encounter many boys and men with the name of Mohammed.

The Jewish tradition, too, places great importance on the name selected for a child. In general, names in the ancient Near East were thought to express a person's true nature. Likewise, the name of a Hebrew child sometimes reflected the conditions that were present when the baby was born—as in the case of Isaac, which means "he will laugh." According to Genesis, Abraham fell to the ground laughing when an angel told him he would have a son, as his wife, Sarah, was well past childbearing years. The narrative also mentions that Sarah quietly laughed when she overheard God's three messengers speaking of her impending pregnancy. Other naming traditions emerged during the period of the Second Temple. Israelites began naming their children after grandparents to maintain family histories, something common in ancient Greek and Egyptian naming traditions.

As tradition teaches us, "A person should be careful in choosing a name for a child that will lead to righteousness" (Tanchuma H'Azinu 7). In the Ashkenazi tradition children are generally named after deceased relatives. I was named Yehiel Moshe after my grandfather, and this was Anglicized to Edgar Miles. The Sephardic tradition permits the use of names of living relatives, though not of living parents. Regardless of these variations, both traditions emphasize that it is important to give the child the name of someone you hold in esteem.

Children born in the Diaspora (outside of Israel) are generally given two names. A Hebrew name reflects their Jewish heritage, and the other name the country in which they were born. In the past, the Jewish name was sometimes a modified form of the child's forebears. Sometimes the link is obvious, other times less so. In the Diaspora, the non-Jewish name is the one featured on the birth certificate, while the Hebrew or, in the past, Yiddish name is used in Jewish events. There are a wide variety of choices for the Hebrew name. Names might derive from the Bible—Eve in lieu of Chava. The Jewish name can also be linked in meaning to the non-Jewish name—a non-Jewish name like Lily or Susan finds its Hebrew counterpart in Shoshana. Modern Hebrew naming traditions, like many world customs, often employ names with symbolic meanings; for example, common male names are Ari and Dov, meaning lion and bear, respectively.

Traditionally, boys are given a name as part of their *brit milah*, the ceremony during which they are circumcised. Circumcision is practiced by most Jews, and in the United States many non-Jews as well, mostly because it has traditionally been associated with good hygiene. But while some research points to hygienic benefits, hygienic concerns were not at the origin of the custom. For the ancient Israelites, the removal of the foreskin of an eight-day-old male infant was a way to symbolically mark the covenant between God and the Jewish people. And as with most Jewish traditions, a festive meal followed the ritual.

As a secular Jew, I do not believe that such physical marking is needed to link us to our people, though I would not be particularly happy if my grandsons were left uncircumcised. Fortunately, it seems science is on my side. Recent studies show that the health benefits of circumcision are greater than its risks.

Traditionally, Ashkenazi Jews tend to announce a baby girl's name on the first *Shabbat* or Torah reading after her birth.

Sephardi Jews often tie the baby naming to the Torah reading as well, reading a verse from the Song of Songs, though in some Sephardi traditions girls are only named at home.

American Jews have developed new customs around baby naming. Some plant trees, link the naming ceremony to a community service project, or light candles. Others adapt the traditional rituals of the *brit milah*, choosing which elements to maintain and which to modify or omit. For nonreligious Jews, the naming ceremony is a beautiful opportunity to welcome a baby into the family of the Jewish people, whether or not you believe in a God-created covenant. In ceremonies for girls, some substitute the ritual circumcision with another physical action, like washing a baby's feet, which echoes an ancient mode of welcome practiced by Abraham. Whatever the ritual, the core of the naming event for both boys and girls is for the parents to announce the child's names and share their hopes and dreams.

BAR AND BAT MITZVAH

I celebrated my *bar mitzvah* on a beautiful Saturday in June 1942. Since that day coincided with my parents' anniversary, my Jewish coming-of-age ceremony also marked twenty years since they had become husband and wife.

As the great day approached, I grew increasingly aware of my Jewishness. I even wanted to be called Edgar Moses instead of Edgar Miles, reflecting the fact that my Hebrew name meant Moses in English. And I was proud of my parents' *bar mitzvah* gift: In my name they had donated an ambulance for the war effort.

During the ceremony, I belted out my portion of the service with vigor even though my voice, in keeping with *bar mitzvah* tradition, was breaking. When I stood beneath the raised platform and the rabbi, whom I loved, pronounced the traditional blessing, I felt a deep sense of awe and a connection to something much larger than myself.

That awe stayed with me throughout the festivities that followed. My cousin Allan Bronfman had baked me a forty-pound fruitcake, and in honor of my parents' anniversary we were allowed to stay up very late to celebrate with them under the starry sky. I can still hear the songs the band played that night: "Moonlight Cocktail," "A Sleepy Lagoon," and "Don't Fence Me In."

A *bar mitzvah*—as mine was, and as many celebrations are today—can be a grand affair. In the *shtetls* of Europe, however, and throughout Jewish history, the celebration was much simpler: It was the time when a young man was called to the Torah for the first time and recognized as accountable for his actions. In earlier times, as now, the *bar mitzvah* took place on the first *Shabbat* after a thirteen-year-old boy's birthday. He was called up to say blessings and read the week's Torah portion, since he was now obliged to follow Jewish law. At the end of the service, extra food and wine would be served to celebrate his transformation from innocence to consciousness.

The first American *bat mitzvah*, for girls, was in 1922. This was the ceremony for Judith Kaplan, whose father, Mordecai Kaplan, founded Reconstructionist Judaism. The *bat mitzvah* became a regular feature in the Conservative movement in the 1960s, and in the 1970s the impact of Jewish feminism led movements from Reform to Modern Orthodox to adopt some form of the *bat mitzvah* ceremony.

The *bar* and *bat mitzvah* tradition has evolved into a major celebration of ever-expanding proportions. I am not against grand festivities, but I feel that many of the lavish, over-the-top *bar* and *bat mitzvahs* of today have gone too far with their emphasis on material display. Crucially, they miss the point of the *bar/bat mitzvah*: to mark the passage from childhood to the moral and ethical responsibilities of adulthood, which are both challenging and fulfilling. As the Talmud teaches, what we strive to overcome is even more valuable than what comes easily to us.

For nonreligious Jews, this coming-of-age ceremony offers an important opportunity to reclaim and reinvent a beautiful Jewish tradition. Too often, the content of the ceremony—the reading of the Torah—is learned by rote, with little attention to the meaning of the text. For Jews who already feel distant from their heritage, this approach has little value. But a thoughtful, questioning engagement with the central text of the Jewish tradition is a very meaningful way to mark an entrance into adulthood. The *bar/bat mitzvah* celebration is also a chance to show a child that he or she is part of a community. It can create a powerful sense of belonging and integration, a sense that one is safe and cared for, because the entire community is expressing joy that the boy or girl is about to join them.

Thoughtful Jews across the religious spectrum are creating new approaches to the *bar/bat mitzvah* ceremony, often expanding them beyond the central ritual of reading from the Torah. A 2013 *New York Times* article reported an initiative within the Reform movement to rethink the *bar/bat mitzvah*, with increased emphasis on creating social action projects. The Workmen's Circle/Arbeter Ring and the Society for Humanistic Judaism both offer a secular *bar/bat mitzvah* program in which each student develops an individualized course of study. Students create projects on diverse topics in Jewish culture and history, interview elderly family members, organize social action projects, and present their work to their communities as talks, performances, or multimedia presentations.

In the past, the *bar/bat mitzvah* was also the time when young Jews began Jewish study in earnest. Unfortunately, today it is just the opposite. Richard Joel, the former head of Hillel International and now the president of Yeshiva University, tells a great joke about a priest, a minister, and a rabbi. The three were commiserating about the mice infesting their houses of worship and sharing various ways they'd tried to rid their sanctuaries of the pests. The priest said he'd hired a flautist at great expense and had the mice piped into a river five miles out of town. Unfortunately, they had returned. The minister described how he'd trapped all the mice and taken them twenty miles away in the countryside and scattered them in the fields. Ten days later, the mice were back. The rabbi then explained his approach. He'd gathered all the mice around him on the *bima* and said, "Congratulations, you are all *bar mitzvahed.*" He then added, "I haven't seen or heard from them since."

The problem, humorously portrayed here, is that all too often the *bar/bat mitzvah* is the end of Jewish involvement. That's a shame, because Judaism provides a rich guide for the many responsibilities a person begins to face when he or she leaves childhood behind. In fact, I think it would be terrific if parents and young people studied jointly and on the day of the *bar/bat mitzvah* proclaimed their commitment to Jewish learning. I believe this is critical, because unless the parents are involved, it is unlikely that the child will remain interested.

MARRIAGE

Not surprisingly, there is no place for celibacy in Judaism. Judaism has always been quite comfortable with the body. I conjecture this might be because of the absence of original sin. Procreation is important, but marriage is not strictly for that purpose. Repeatedly, the tradition underscores the idea that companionship, love, and intimacy are as central to marriage as procreation. Woman was created to be a partner to man, the Bible tells us in one version of the creation story, for "it is not good for man to be alone" (Genesis 2:18).

A deeply sacred act, the Jewish wedding is rich with metaphor and symbolism. As the bride and groom stand together under the canopy with a rabbi and a cantor, it is they who marry each other, pledging their lives one to the other.

The first step in this commitment is the signing of the *ketubah*, a special contract grounded in history. Traditionally, women had no rights to property or inheritance within the Jewish marriage, and they were vulnerable to destitution if their husbands divorced or predeceased them. This changed with the introduction of the *ketubah*, which evolved to provide for the wife.

Through the rich tradition of this document, the bride and groom are linked to every couple in every generation that has married under Jewish law. As an object of Jewish ceremonial art, it is designed to be beautiful, and *ketubot* (plural of *ketubah*) are often are framed and hung in the couple's home. Signed by the groom and witnesses just before the ceremony, the *ketubah* is also practical, as it enumerates the rights and responsibilities of the groom in relation to the bride. It answers questions such as how the husband will provide food, clothing, and affection. And while there are important differences between prenuptial agreements and the *ketubah*, there are some similarities. One could say that just as the *Shabbat* preceded contemporary labor laws, the *ketubah* might be considered an early form of today's prenups.

This document is read aloud during the ceremony, after the exchange of rings, to mark the transition from betrothal to marriage. Once it is read, the *ketubah* becomes the property of the bride. Like so much in Judaism, the practical and the poetic merge, and there is an intimate relationship between the law and love.

Another beautiful custom at Jewish weddings is the *huppah*, a special wedding canopy that turns any space into a revered or holy place. Open on all sides, it is held aloft over the new couple by family members or friends bearing its poles, evoking the idea that the couple is not alone but live within the embrace of family and community. Some believe it represents the first home of the new couple, and its open structure announces that the couple's home will always be welcoming of guests, in a manner similar to the tent of Abraham and Sarah.

Perhaps the most iconic image of the Jewish wedding is the breaking of the wineglass beneath the groom's heel. As he stomps on it, the wedding guests shout, *"Mazel tov!"* (a phrase said to express congratulations or wish someone good luck). This custom has come to mean many things over generations, the most common one being the destruction of the Temple. To me, however, the broken glass is a reminder that even in the midst of our happiness we should not forget the shattered pieces of the world.

Today, traditional Jewish marriage customs are being adapted and embraced by many, including increasing numbers of gay and lesbian couples. Keshet, the organization started by Bronfman Fellowships alumna Idit Klein, beautifully articulates what it means to adapt traditional rituals in its Marriage

Project, an online resource on Jewish weddings for LGBTQ couples. The description of the project quotes Isaiah, who preached:

> Widen the place of your tent,
> Stretch the curtains of your dwellings—stint not!
> Lengthen your cords, and strengthen your stakes.
>   (Isaiah 54:2)

The website goes on to explain:

> The image is of a tent flexible enough to expand to contain those who had not been included in the past—but also capable of rooting itself in the soil of Jewish law, culture, and tradition—so it does not remain too loose to be able to stand firm. Our established and created rituals are the places in which we dwell and create meaning, and the strength of our future community is grounded within them.

CREATING A JEWISH HOME

The presence of objects with Jewish significance is a wonderful way to make the home a meaningful dwelling place. One might begin by placing a *mezuzah*, meaning "doorpost," at the entrance to a home. The *mezuzah* is the tiny piece of inscribed parchment, usually within a decorated outer casing. The origin of this idea comes from a passage in Deuteronomy that instructs Jews to affix the words of the *Shema Yisrael* prayer—a prayer that asserts the idea that God is one and indivisible—on their doorposts.

For nonreligious Jews, this custom can be a meaningful way to assert the enduring importance of Judaism and to remind yourself and your family that entering a home means entering a space of beauty and meaning. While the traditional *mezuzah* contains the *Shema* prayer, one might substitute it with another poem, or perhaps vary the parchment slip, inserting a different Jewish value to be discussed each month. With a bit of inventiveness, the *mezuzah* could become a rich source of Jewish learning. Children love surprises, and discovering the tiny parchment message secretly tucked inside the decorative casing could become a meaningful—and cherished—family ritual.

Another of Judaism's most iconic symbols is the candelabrum known as a *menorah*. The *menorah* is widely considered an emblem of *Hanukkah*, whose central image is the eight-branched candelabra with the ninth holder called the "servant," as it is the candle used to light all the others. But the history of the ritual object derives from the seven-branched *menorah* used in the Temple and described in Exodus, where construction details lay out the steps involved in the creation of each element.

In the *midrashic* account, the exacting instructions left Moses at a loss, and despite God's repeated attempts to help—including drawing a *menorah* of fire in the air—Moses could not grasp them. Finally, God despaired of Moses and told him to ask the artist Bezalel to make it. According to tradition, Bezalel finished the task with ease. Our sages attributed these words to Moses: "God showed me the menorah design many times, but I could not fashion it. But you, without being shown, succeeded from your own knowledge. You must have stood b'tzel-el—in the shadow of God—and watched while God showed me how to make it" (Genesis Rabbah 15:10). I like this fanciful tale because it places creativity squarely in human hands. It also appeals to me because sages suggested that two forces—the rational and the imaginative—are needed to bring things of beauty, power, and meaning into the world. This fits with the Jewish tradition's openness to creative interpretation.

After the destruction of the Temple, the *menorah* was created with six branches to avoid exact duplication of Temple items, and it has since become an enduring symbol. The *menorah* also reflects Israel's mission to be "a light unto the nations" (Isaiah 42:6). While many Jews find this a discomfiting notion—why should any group of people or any one nation be a beacon to others?—it is important to remember that the moral laws received at Sinai, not the people, are the lights. The people are simply the messengers, the ones who chose or were chosen to deliver the message. The light of the law belongs to all.

Given these scriptural ideas, the *menorah* is rich with possibilities for interpretation. When I see its lights, I remind myself that as a human being I am charged with the responsibility of carrying justice—in big ways and small—into our too often benighted world.

Beyond objects for the home, I urge you to explore if you are a parent, or might one day become a parent, the beautiful tradition of the *birchat*, or blessing of the children. This ritual takes place every *Shabbat*, as we celebrate the dignity of rest.

During the traditional blessing, parents ask God to grant their children grace and protection. For religious and non-religious parents, the blessing is a beautiful chance to share our wishes and dreams for our children. The blessing can provide parents with the opportunity to seriously reflect on what it really means to be the life guardian of a child. Besides their physical beings, what else are we guarding? What values are we meant to instill? What emotional, spiritual, and intellectual gifts do we want to give them?

The blessing can also provide an opportunity for developing a child's sense of his or her heritage. For thousands of years, parents asked that their sons be like Ephraim and Menashe—the sons of Joseph who were the first brothers in the Bible to be without rivalry—and their daughters like the mothers of our people: Sarah, Rebecca, Rachel, and Leah. This is a great opportunity to remind children that they are part of a long and vibrant history that stretches back thousands of years.

Parents might also take the opportunity to seek out their own role models among Jewish history and culture and write an original blessing. The blessing might also be used to impart some particular triumph or achievement of nonbiblical heroes and heroines for the purpose of inculcating a sense of pride. Of course role models should be drawn from a wide range of cultures, but why not include some members of one's own?

SHIVAH

When a parent, child, sibling, or spouse dies, the effect on the bereaved can be overwhelming. Losing a family member can feel unbearable, and some struggle painfully to imagine how their lives will continue without their loved one. Even when the bereaved was not close to the deceased, many emotions come crowding in: regret, guilt, anger, and the sadness of opportunities missed.

The Jewish custom of sitting *shivah*, a Hebrew word meaning "seven," is designed to help both those who were very close to the deceased and those who, for whatever reason, had become distant from the one who has passed away. *Shivah* is a psychologically powerful custom that serves many purposes and is remarkable for its deep insight into the human mind and the needs of a mourner.

In the case of someone who can barely cope with the new reality, the structure created by *shivah* does not allow much time or opportunity for brooding. Rather, it forces the person to direct attention to other matters. For seven days there is a constant stream of visitors, some welcome, others less so, and some perhaps not even familiar. The many visitors may inspire gratitude or annoyance, depending on the situation and the personalities involved. Either way, they are both a distraction and an outlet.

The custom of *shivah* also allows the mourner to be the center of attention for a week. The message is clear: You are still part of the community; we care about you; your loss makes us sad. And mourners need attention because all their energy is directed toward the emotional turmoil of loss.

In traditional observations of *shivah*, mourners stay in the house. Guests bring food and leave it in the kitchen. Mourners do not shave or cut their hair. These customs show a deep understanding of the psychology of bereavement. A person in shock will easily forget to eat and to look after themselves. But with food in the house and guests coming in, all our social instincts come to the fore. Food is nibbled, basic washing is performed, but not too much is demanded. The custom of partial grooming forces people not to deviate too far from their ordinary habits but at the same time limits the pressure on them. During this period of grief, mourners should not be concerned with how they look, nor should they be expected to look their best at a time when they feel their worst. This is one explanation for the commonly observed custom of covering mirrors.

In a form of reverse psychology, being shut indoors for a week causes the mind to rebel against the confinement, and the first time the mourner ventures outdoors after the seven-day period, there can be a sense of the comfort in the beauty life still has to offer. The world looks different after being indoors for a week, and it is different now that a close person is gone.

For thirty days from the time of the burial the mourner continues to have restrictions, and does not attend parties or public events. That is the end of official mourning in all deaths other than parents', in which case mourning continues for a year. When it comes to rituals surrounding death, lenience is prescribed in all legal matters that are uncertain. This sensitivity is a remarkable aspect of Jewish mourning.

Today it is not always possible to sit *shivah* for seven days. People must return to work. Thus the *shivah* ritual is often shortened to three days, or to three days and only a part of the day for the remaining four. However, depending on the level of trauma, a person may not be able to return to work, and that is when the full seven days are often lifesavers, perhaps literally.

But we cannot stop living even if we want to. The community rallies to help the mourners and bring them back into the world of the living. The emphasis on limiting mourning in Judaism is not surprising given its emphasis on life. As noted in the Torah, choosing life is the Jewish way. One might even say that "To life!" is the Jewish mantra. And yet the deceased is never forgotten. Once a year, we light a *yarzheit* candle—in Yiddish called a "soul" candle—on the anniversary of a death. This yearly ritual commemorates the departed and reminds us how our loved ones live on in the good deeds they performed, and in our hearts.

CHAPTER 6

One Big Family

Judaism will have to be conceived as a noncreedal religious civilization centered in loyalty to the body of the Jewish people throughout the world.

—Mordecai Kaplan

ONE OF THE CENTRAL ASSUMPTIONS OF JUDAISM IS that all Jews, whatever their cultural roots, are bound by shared history, stories, beliefs, and practices. This concept is traditionally referred to as *klal Israel* (all of Israel) and, more recently, as Jewish peoplehood. It includes those who join the Jewish people by choice as well as by birth.

Many have debated the best term for Judaism—is it a culture, an ethnicity, a religion, or a civilization? I would say all and none of the above. My own feeling is that Judaism is a big family of individuals with a common bond that has stayed strong through a long history and much hardship. Those who want to become part of this story are Jews too. I believe the tent should be open and welcoming to anyone who wishes to join.

For younger Jews today, choosing a particular ethnicity or culture may seem too narrow a form of self-identification. But I do not see Judaism as a form of tribalism that divides rather than unites. The Jewish people are one of the many vibrant patches on the richly diverse quilt of humanity. Each patch has its own design, and together they make a beautiful whole. Embracing your heritage deepens your understanding of who you are and where you come from and brings you into a more meaningful relationship with the multicultural world.

To identify with the Jewish people does not mean to care only for the fates of other Jews. In fact, the opposite is true. The Jewish tradition, from ancient to modern times, has always placed tremendous emphasis on protecting and caring for those who are different. Repeatedly, the Hebrew Bible assigns us the responsibility of taking care of the stranger, reminding us, "You shall not oppress the stranger, for you know the feelings of the stranger, having yourselves been strangers in the land of Egypt" (Exodus 23:9). The idea is so central to Judaism that it threads throughout the whole Hebrew Bible. We hear it in Leviticus and in the prophetic texts of Zechariah and Jeremiah. The Talmud, too, cites many cases where concern for non-Jews is just as important, and in some cases takes precedence over the care of one's own people. Our sages taught, "We sustain the non-Jewish poor with the Jewish poor, visit the non-Jewish sick with the Jewish sick, and bury the non-Jewish dead with the Jewish dead, for the sake of peace" (Gittin 61a).

All of this said, I remain a strong proponent of Jews helping Jews. In the words of the great sage Hillel, "If I am not for myself, who will be for me? But if I am only for myself, who am I? If not now, when?" (*Pirkei Avot* 1:14).

Jews have long felt a responsibility for one another. Because the world was often so hostile, throughout history Jews tended to live in tight communities and rely on each other in times of need and crisis. This interdependence is a beautiful thing, and it is one of the benefits of belonging—whether by birth or by choice—to the Jewish people.

I grew up with a sense of shared concern for the welfare of other Jews. Despite my own distance from Jewish texts and traditions as a younger man, it was the notion of Jewish peoplehood that motivated me to become the president of the World Jewish Congress, an organization dedicated to the interests and security of the Jewish people. My deep sense of peoplehood gave me the fortitude to fight the difficult battles to secure the freedom of Soviet Jews and to help recover Jewish assets stolen by the Nazis. It inspired me to relentlessly advocate with President George H. W. Bush in order to persuade him to help undo the 1972 UN resolution equating Zionism with racism. And it was peoplehood that fueled my quest to convince the Spanish and German governments to recognize or live up to their responsibilities to Israel. All of these were very big battles, but as a Jew I felt duty-bound to wage them.

Throughout Jewish history, one finds individuals who have dedicated their lives to helping their fellow Jews. In sixteenth-century Portugal, Doña Gracia Nasi (also known by her Christian name, Beatriz de Luna Miquez) spent a good deal of her life and money to help save Jews from the terror of the Spanish Inquisition. As a young wealthy *conversa*, a Jew whose family had been forced to convert to Catholicism, she organized an embargo and built synagogues and yeshivas to help *conversos* learn about the ancient faith they had once abandoned in fear.

Another person who epitomizes the idea of Jews helping Jews is Emma Lazarus. Born into a wealthy Sephardic family in 1849, Lazarus was recognized early for her gifts as a poet, publishing her first volume of verse at age seventeen. When Jews escaping the pogroms and hardship of Eastern Europe began flooding into New York City, she worked tirelessly on their behalf, advocating for justice and helping them build new lives. One of her key accomplishments was to help her fellow Jews develop vocational skills through the establishment of the Hebrew Technical Institute. Her devotion to helping struggling immigrants, Jewish and non-Jewish, is expressed in her famous sonnet "The New Colossus," which is engraved on a plaque mounted inside the pedestal of the Statue of Liberty:

> Not like the brazen giant of Greek fame,
> With conquering limbs astride from land to land;
> Here at our sea-washed, sunset gates shall stand

A mighty woman with a torch, whose flame
Is the imprisoned lightning, and her name
Mother of Exiles. From her beacon-hand
Glows world-wide welcome; her mild eyes command
The air-bridged harbor that twin cities frame.
"Keep, ancient lands, your storied pomp!" cries she
With silent lips. "Give me your tired, your poor,
Your huddled masses yearning to breathe free,
The wretched refuse of your teeming shore.
Send these, the homeless, tempest-tost to me,
I lift my lamp beside the golden door!"

The idea of Jewish peoplehood was not universally embraced by Lazarus's fellow Jews. She was furious with the many wealthy Jews of her highly educated Sephardic community who, along with the upper-class German Jews, were embarrassed by the less sophisticated and bedraggled Jews of Russian and Polish descent pouring into Lower Manhattan. Not to be outdone, some Eastern European Jews were contemptuous of the Syrian Jews who first settled in Manhattan's Lower East Side in the early 1900s. Today, Jewish cultures and communities are still divided by discord and animosity.

Still, when push comes to shove, Jews tend to support Jews. It was a feeling of kinship with the Jewish people that no doubt motivated Judy Feld Carr, a Canadian human rights activist and musicologist, to spend twenty-eight years of her life helping thousands of Syrian Jews reach the safer shores of Canada,

America, and Israel. And it's what led the Israeli government to mount Operation Moses in 1984 and Operation Solomon in 1991 to rescue Ethiopian Jewish communities from their drought-stricken land. More recently, Jewish organizations are rallying around French Jews who have been experiencing a spike in anti-Semitic attacks.

It's hard to know what creates this family feeling among Jews. It might be that our Jewish story begins with a father and mother, Abraham and Sarah. The ancient kabbalists (practitioners of a mystical form of Judaism) explain the Jewish people as a unity of souls. I don't buy into the notion of souls, and even if I did, there is certainly no difference between Jewish and non-Jewish souls, as Maimonides rightfully points out. Most likely, the sense of familial connection is the result of thousands of years of shared history and practices. But whatever the explanation, Jews often feel like members of an extended family.

This has it pluses and minuses. Because we are so closely identified, Jews, particularly in my generation, tend to be acutely aware of the failings and sufferings, triumphs and achievements of fellow Jews. Like any other people, we have our share of criminals, con men, thieves, and everyday individuals who, if not bona fide lawbreakers, fall short of the high bar of moral and ethical excellence Judaism demands of its followers. In fact, Yiddish has a rich vocabulary identifying all sorts of scoundrels, *gonif* and *shuyster* being two of the more familiar terms. We often feel a sense of collective joy or shame when Jews shine or behave in egregious ways. One only has to think of the murder of Israel's prime minister Yitzhak Rabin by a fellow Jew, or the financial crimes of Bernie Madoff. By the same token, we feel pride when we think of Jews like Albert Einstein and Jonas Salk.

The sense of family bond among Jews around the world can seem remarkable to non-Jews. I experienced this first-hand when, during my tenure as president of the World Jewish Congress, I was in Bucharest for a series of meetings. Just as I was preparing to leave, I was asked to make a call to the Romanian foreign minister. It seemed a Jewish man was about to be executed in Iran. The Romanian diplomat I was to contact had a good relationship with the Iranian government, so the plan was for me to enlist his help in the hope of reversing the order.

When I reached him, the Romanian official seemed perplexed. "Do you know this guy?" he asked. "Is he a relative?"

"I don't know him," I answered, "but he's a Jew and all Jews care for each other." The answer seemed to both fascinate and confuse him, but he made the call, and a stay of execution resulted.

While perhaps more prominent among older Jews, the sense of peoplehood is striking among youth as well. In 1994, I visited a Jewish educational institution in a poor neighborhood in Buenos Aires after the tragic bombing of a Jewish charity. As many believed the attack had been perpetrated by Iranian terrorists seeking to demolish the unfolding peace process in the Middle East, I asked the assembled children and adults to say not only, "The Jewish people live," but also, "The Jewish people live in peace." The kids then sang and presented works they'd created. Almost every project expressed the children's sorrow for the victims and their determination not to allow this destruction to dissuade them from embracing their heritage. I felt deeply connected to every one of those strong, proud, resolute children.

One of the most wonderful ways to celebrate Jewish peoplehood is through observation of Jewish holidays. There is, for example, something very moving in the thought that when we sit down to the Passover Seder, Jews all over the world are doing the same. And although Seder customs have changed over the millennia, and vary between Jewish communities, I find great comfort in knowing that the central elements of the ancient ritual have persisted. The festivals observed by Jews throughout history and around the world connect us to the great chain of our tradition, as each one with its unique theme and customs brings key Jewish ideas to life.

Part III

CHAPTER 7

Reason to Celebrate

God appointed the Sabbath and holidays as among the strongest means for preserving the Jewish people's identity and character.

—Judah HaLevi, Sefer HaKuzari, 3:10

The festivals are all for rejoicing and pleasurable gatherings.

—Moses Maimonides, *The Guide of the Perplexed*, 3:43

LIKE ALL HOLIDAYS, THE JEWISH CELEBRATIONS PROvide us with the chance to step away from the tasks and chores of quotidian life. But rather than being an escape from our responsibilities, our festivals are an opportunity to delve deeper into the important things that can get lost in the bustle of everyday living. Jewish holidays are not stand-alone events; their position in the cycle of the year yields a rich message. Each Jewish celebration is about renewal, recognizing that joy often follows on the heels of sadness. For instance, after *Yom*

Kippur, we know the bounty of *Sukkot*; after the harrowing escape from Egypt, we receive the greatest gift of all: the laws that transformed the lives of billions of people. The Jewish holidays, like the Seder meal, pair the bitter and the sweet, the tragic and the triumphant. This is one of the things I love so much about Judaism. Along with the emphasis on questioning and insistence on ethical behavior, it is realistic—sometimes painfully so—about the human experience.

Having evolved over millennia, all the holidays possess rich and varied histories, meanings, and symbols. For skeptical Jews who regard observing the holidays as a choice, not a commandment, the reasons to celebrate are many and deep.

Given the overall number, and the exacting details that apply to each, I understand that to practice all in a traditional way is probably beyond the interest of the average person. It certainly is beyond mine. Therefore, in this chapter I have chosen to focus on a selection of holidays whose traditions and themes are particularly relevant to the questions and concerns of Jews today. I have set apart discussion of Passover, the holiday that embodies all that I value in Judaism, in a separate chapter.

For more in-depth information on the holidays and life-cycle events touched on in this book, as well as those omitted, I recommend a visit to MyJewishLearning.com, a website initiated by The Samuel Bronfman Foundation that serves as a rich resource for those who wish to expand and deepen their Jewish knowledge and practice.

SHABBAT

Derived from the Hebrew word that means to rest or cease from activity, *Shabbat* is a holiday I've come to greatly respect and enjoy, though it certainly wasn't that way as a child. On Friday night, my mother, my father, and my siblings and I would gather in our home's formal oak dining room. Despite the crystal chandelier overhead and a stretch of windows, the room felt oppressive to me. Some of the gloomy feeling came from the physical environment itself. There was an oversized table on one end where my father often carved, and above his chair hung his portrait, stern and somber, by the Canadian artist Alphonse Jongers.

The table seating didn't contribute to a warm feeling either. My brother and I were located on each side of Father, and the girls with Mother at the opposite end of the table. Even as a young boy, I found this arrangement strange, as it sent out the message that Mother was in charge of the girls, and Father the boys.

The mood might have been lightened a bit and inter-generational ties strengthened if my parents had explained the meaning of the various *Shabbat* rituals to us—the candle lighting, the blessing of the wine and bread. But none of that happened. Instead, we were held hostage to Father's endless recitals of "lessons in life." Though in retrospect I admire his desire to impart what he valued to his children, as a young man I found it tedious. Things got no better on

Saturday. We had to attend a dull junior congregation, which separated us from my friends who were out and about. All of these factors turned the *Shabbat* of my childhood into more of an endurance test than a day of rest, and obscured the fact that *Shabbat* is one of the greatest gifts the world has ever received.

The concept of *Shabbat* comes from the idea in Genesis that God created the world in six days and rested on the seventh. As we learn in Exodus:

> Remember the sabbath day and keep it holy. Six days you shall labor and do all your work, but the seventh day is a sabbath of the Lord your God: you shall not do any work—you, your son or daughter, your male or female slave, or your cattle, or the stranger who is within your settlements. For in six days the Lord made heaven and earth and sea, and all that is in them, and He rested on the seventh day; therefore, the Lord blessed the sabbath day and hallowed it. (Exodus 20:8–11)

But there is more to *Shabbat* than this usual explanation. In the book of Deuteronomy we are instructed to remember that because we were once slaves in Egypt who were freed by the mighty hand and outstretched arm of God, we are commanded to observe *Shabbat*. Because of this, *Shabbat*, like Passover, becomes a time for us to remember that unlike slaves, we have the privilege of rest. A *midrash* on this theme tells us that when Moses saw the slaves toiling without rest, he went to Pharaoh and pleaded their case. Moses wisely made his case by appealing to logic, not emotions, as he is often shown as doing in traditional sources. Without rest, he told Pharaoh, the slaves would die. Pharaoh told Moses to do as he wished, and so as prince of Egypt, Moses instituted the seventh day for rest (Exodus Rabbah 1:28).

In the more mystical branches of Judaism, *Shabbat* is sometimes referred to as a bride or a queen. In ancient times, our sages would dress in white garments and wander the hills, calling out for their bride, an idea that inspired the liturgical poem "Come My Beloved," a welcoming song that some Jewish communities sing as part of Friday night services. In Jewish literature, art, and poetry, *Shabbat* is also sometimes portrayed as the feminine aspect of God, known as *Shekhina*.

As a secular Jew, I regard this concept as a way to celebrate the nurturing and embracing qualities that are traditionally associated with the feminine, like the concept of yin (feminine) and yang (masculine) in Chinese philosophy. When viewed through this metaphorical prism, *Shabbat* can be seen as a chance to "wed" the different sides of our selves.

Traditionally, *Shabbat* begins no later than eighteen minutes before sunset on Friday evening and ends when three evening stars appear in Saturday's sky. The celebratory period includes three festive meals: one on Friday evening, another on Saturday morning, and the concluding one late on Saturday afternoon.

Two candles are lit at the start of *Shabbat*, in accordance with rabbinic law. Legal mandates aside, I see much resonance in this tradition. Sometimes the twin candles instruct me to act from the head and heart; other times I imagine them as symbols for the two tablets of the law, which in turn prompts me to thank my ancestors for helping the world understand that without responsibilities there can be no freedom.

Following the candle lighting, the Friday night meal begins with *kiddush*, a blessing or prayer that sanctifies the wine we drink from a special cup, which is often silver or bronze, but could be any nice cup. This is followed by the *Hamotzi*, or blessing over the bread. On *Shabbat*, we use two loaves of challah, the puffy, egg-rich bread of Eastern European, or Ashkenazi, traditions. Non-Ashkenazi Jews use a different loaf, generally eggless, that resembles biblical showbread, the consecrated unleavened bread placed by the ancient Israeli priests on a sanctuary table on *Shabbat*.

In the Ashkenazi tradition the bread is covered. Some believe this is to protect it from inferior status due to its secondary position in the Friday night blessing lineup. Bread, of course, doesn't have feelings, but as with many Jewish traditions, it is an apt metaphor to remind us not to insult other people and to be sensitive to those who might be positioned on the lower rungs of life's too often hierarchical arrangements.

These double loaves have also been seen as symbolizing the double portion of manna that fell from the sky during the Exodus from Egypt, ensuring that the ancient Israelites would not have to forage for food on *Shabbat*. Through this, we are reminded that we are fortunate to be part of a long tradition of people who, after much struggle, are now free.

Shabbat closes with a symbolic *Havdalah*, or parting, ceremony that, depending on your cultural tradition, involves overflowing cups of sweet wine and the fragrance of spices through the air. I love the traditional *Havdalah* prayer that children at Jewish summer camps often sing by a lake. The melody blends the sadness of farewell with the joy of celebrating the moment, with all the senses engaged.

Shabbat, above all, underscores the idea that "being" is as important as "doing." As Abraham Joshua Heschel beautifully describes in his masterpiece, *The Sabbath*:

To set apart one day a week for freedom, a day on which we would not use the instruments which have been so easily turned into weapons of destruction, a day for being with ourselves, a day of detachment from the vulgar, of independence of external obligations, a day on which we stop worshipping the idols of technical civilization, a day on which we use no money, a day of armistice in the economic struggle with our fellow men and the forces of nature—is there any institution that holds out a greater hope for man's progress than the Sabbath?

Heschel's words perfectly capture the spirit of *Shabbat*. With its candle lighting, traditional meals with family and friends, and parting ceremony, it is a wonderful antidote to today's fast-paced world. To quote Heschel again, it is a "cathedral in time" that "neither the Romans nor the Germans were able to burn."

Shabbat is also the perfect opportunity for unplugging from our 24/7 connected reality. The group Reboot, a network of young, creative Jews who have sought ways to grapple with questions of Jewish identity and community in terms that will be meaningful to their generation, wrote up a ten-point Shabbat Manifesto to drive this point home. The manifesto, while open-ended, is inspired and informed by traditional *Shabbat* concepts. It is a first-class example of young Jews taking tradition into their own hands and shaping it into something that complements today's realities:

Avoid technology.
Connect with loved ones.
Nurture your health.
Get outside.
Avoid commerce.
Light candles.
Drink wine.
Eat bread.
Find silence.
Give back.

For both the religious and nonreligious, *Shabbat* provides us with a rich opportunity to assess our actions of the past week while making plans for the week ahead. I love the idea of studying our sacred texts, philosophy, and other Jewish literature with my children and grandchildren. Freed of the demands of the marketplace, we can turn our attention to the marketplace of ideas.

Just as important, *Shabbat* provides us a chance to reconnect with the beauties of nature. In his sonnet "The World Is Too Much with Us," the nineteenth-century poet William Wordsworth expresses his belief that the more developed parts of ourselves, which some identify as the spiritual side, cannot thrive without a connection to nature:

> Getting and spending, we lay waste our powers:
> Little we see in Nature that is ours;
> We have given our hearts away, a sordid boon!
> This Sea that bares her bosom to the moon;
> The winds that will be howling at all hours,
> And are up-gathered now like sleeping flowers;
> For this, for everything, we are out of tune;
> It moves us not.

The enduring tradition of *Shabbat* helps us understand that life is always best when lived in balance and provides us with a beautiful weekly space to rest, reflect, and recalibrate.

THE HIGH HOLIDAYS

The High Holidays begin with *Rosh Hashanah*—the New Year—and end with *Yom Kippur*, the Day of Atonement. This ten-day period is often known as the Days of Awe or the Ten Days of Repentance. It is the time when Jews are called upon to evaluate themselves and their behavior over the past year and to dedicate themselves to the hard work of redeeming their relationships with other human beings. During the month of Elul, which precedes *Rosh Hashanah*, and throughout the ten days between *Rosh Hashanah* and *Yom Kippur*, we focus on shedding our illusions and casting aside the justifications we have made for ourselves.

During this time we engage in a process known as *teshuvah*, a word that literally means "turning," though it is often translated as "repentance." This rigorous self-inquiry must be followed by a process, known as *mehila*, of seeking forgiveness from those we may have hurt. As a secular Jew I find this tradition rewarding and challenging. Praying to the heavens above is often much easier than wrestling with oneself and admitting one has done wrong. Prayer and self-reflection are both required in Judaism, but I think asking forgiveness from other people is the more challenging task.

This can be especially true within families. The company I headed for twenty-three years, Seagram, was a family business. Family businesses, while wonderful enterprises, come with their own set of complexities, and there is little division between the personal and the political. My father built Seagram from the ground up, and my brother Charles and I often were placed against each other in competitive roles. As a result, our relationship was tense for many years, each of us seeking our father's approval as he compared us to each other. Although the growing divide between us was not technically either of our faults, I acknowledge that as a young man I did little to make it better.

After our father died, I became Seagram's chief executive officer, and Charles was my partner. At times I treated him poorly, neglecting to consult with him on major decisions. Naturally, he resented it. Because I did not fully consult with my brother or engage him on critical decisions, I sometimes misjudged or avoided business deals and investment opportunities. Years later, when Charles and I were on good terms again, I apologized to him. That apology required complete honesty. Life would have gone on serenely for both of us without the apology, but sometimes doing nothing is as wrong as the act itself. I knew deep within myself that I needed to make amends.

The Days of Awe can be a time to heal rifts within families and to engage in the kind of open dialogue that can prevent them from occurring. This period is an excellent time for a family to sit down to dinner and, with the purpose of forgiveness, go around the table discussing whose action hurt whom. This could help to make our families closer and more careful about how we treat each other. We may not have much say over "who lives or dies," in the words of the traditional prayer, but we do have control over our behavior and our hearts.

Rosh Hashanah: Birthday of the World

The Days of Awe begin with *Rosh Hashanah*, which in Hebrew means literally "head of the year." As with every major Jewish holiday, at *Rosh Hashanah* we light the candles in the evening, recite *kiddush* to sanctify the wine, and bless the bread. We also serve foods that symbolize different aspects of the holiday and amplify its meaning. Many people avoid bitter or sour foods during this period and eat sweet foods, such as apples dipped in honey, which symbolize blessings and spiritual and material abundance. To honor the cycle of the year, challah is often shaped into round loaves.

Interestingly, *Rosh Hashanah*, unlike most other Jewish holidays, has no tie to an event in Jewish history or to an agricultural festival. Instead, its focus is on the concept of transgressions—where we have done wrong, individually or as a community, and what we are going to do about it.

The idea of casting off our transgressions is tied to the custom of *tashlich*, an ancient and curious practice where participants toss bread into rivers, ponds, lakes, or other bodies of water. There are many explanations for this, from water being where Jewish kings were crowned, making it the proper element to visit on the day when God is crowned king, to appeasing devils. The symbol that most captures my imagination is about the fish that swim where the crumbs are tossed.

As fish have no eyelids, their eyes never close. To religious Jews, this corresponds to God's watchful presence. As a secular Jew, I see *tashlich* as a reminder to keep my own eyes open to my failings.

Another custom of the High Holidays is the blowing of the shofar. This three-thousand-year-old musical instrument is made from a horn of a kosher animal, such as the ram, antelope, gazelle, or goat. The ram's horn is associated with the story of the binding of Isaac, a biblical narrative read in synagogue during the holiday. When Abraham, the father of the Jewish people, is commanded to sacrifice his beloved son Isaac on the altar, he makes preparations to fulfill the order. But at the last minute, an angel pulls back his hand, and the boy is saved. The shofar is thought by many to symbolize the horn of the ram that, in Genesis, God substituted for Isaac at the last moment.

To me, this story is confounding. It stands in stark contrast to the fact that Judaism teaches the wrongness of murder, and is further complicated by the fact that God had earlier told Abraham that through his own son Isaac, his people would be as numerous as the stars. The only way this story makes sense to me is to try to find within it a metaphor about human behavior. Perhaps we could interpret the angel staying Abraham's hand to mean that when we deeply listen we will hear a voice—some call it conscience—that tells us it is wrong to "sacrifice" our own children for any reason, from professional demands to self-absorption.

However one chooses to understand its role in this perplexing story, the shofar has become a quintessential symbol of the Jewish people and of the Jewish New Year. In the Ashkenazi tradition, on *Rosh Hashanah* the shofar is sounded one hundred times. When I first heard those repetitive blasts I found myself getting bored. But as has been the case throughout my Jewish journey, the more I learned, the more interesting things became.

There has been much discussion of the meaning of the sounds of the shofar, whose "music" runs from a first long note (*tekiah*), to a three-note broken sound (*shvarim*), to nine rapidly performed staccato notes (*teruah*). Maimonides heard the shofar blasts as a wake-up call, an insistent alarm that alerts us to the importance of the day. Other sages interpreted the sounds as three different types of human cries. My own reaction blends Maimonides' assertion with those of other sages. To my imagination, the long straight note calls attention to the moral and ethical tasks at hand; the three short sounds evoke the sound of sobbing, perhaps reflecting the voices of those whose forgiveness I need to seek; and the nine rapidly played notes at the end of each section remind me of the urgency of it all.

Typically, the quarrelsome rabbis of old could not reach an agreement on what was the most authentic shofar sound. The long blast? The three shorter blasts? The nine rapid-fire tones? And in what order should all these blasts come together? Unable to arrive at a single answer, they decided to group the sounds in various ways. Without detailing their system, they managed to cover all possible configurations with one hundred blasts. When I learned the story of the various blasts, I felt proud of our tradition's flexibility, its inclusiveness, and its desire to make all opinions and voices count. That said, for me, fewer blasts would be a welcome revision!

Yet another element of *Rosh Hashanah* is the concept of the three heavenly books that are opened on the first day of *Rosh Hashanah* and closed on *Yom Kippur.* The poetically charged idea of God inscribing our names and our fates into heavenly books is what is behind the oft-heard greeting at this time, "May you be inscribed and sealed for a good year."

I find it highly improbable that the concept of these mysterious books was ever intended to be anything other than a metaphor, perhaps inspired by poetically charged lines in the book of Revelation:

And I saw the dead, small and great, stand before God; and the books were opened: and another book was opened, which is the book of life: and the dead were judged out of those things which were written in the books, according to their works. (20:12)

Still, it is a wonderful image and one that could inspire contemporary practices. As a way of taking stock of our behavior, we might create physical New Year books. Such books could even become part of an ongoing practice of *tikkun middot*, taking stock of our internal selves.

The idea of the heavenly books runs through the recitation of a poem read during the *Rosh Hashanah* service called *Unetaneh Tokef*, translated as "Let Us Cede Power." A staple of the holidays, this poem was written by an unknown author, probably during the Byzantine period:

> On Rosh Hashanah it is written, and on Yom Kippur
>   it is sealed.
> How many will pass and how many will be created?
>   Who will live and who will die?
> Who in their time and who not in their time? Who by
>   fire and who by water?
> Who by sword and who by beast? Who by hunger and who
>   by thirst?
> Who by earthquake and who by plague? Who by strangling
>   and who by stoning?
> Who will rest and who will wander? Who will be safe
>   and who will be torn?
> Who will be calm and who will be tormented? Who
>   will become poor and who will get rich?
> Who will be made humble and who will be raised up?
> But teshuvah and tefilah and tzedakah deflect the evil
>   of the decree.

The poem's focus is on the day when we are judged. But despite its raw terror and assertion that no one can know the future—either our own or that of our fellows—Judaism, ever positive, tells us there is hope. The poem teaches us that through asking forgiveness, prayer, and the giving of charity, the severity of the outcome is lessened or deflected. We have the ability to change and we are responsible for behaving ethically—not because we will be punished or rewarded, but because it is the right thing to do.

Yom Kippur: Day of Atonement

The High Holidays reach their apotheosis on *Yom Kippur*, the holiest day of the Jewish year. It comes at the end of the Days of Awe, and bears the chief theme of "afflicting" ourselves for the purpose of achieving reverence and repentance. Like Passover, *Yom Kippur* is tied to the events that occurred at Mount Sinai, and many of its rituals symbolically reflect the story's scene in which Moses prepares to receive the law.

On this day, we do not eat or drink. We ignore our physical needs to better focus on our spiritual concerns. Some people also wear white clothing to express the moral purity they seek, a practice that might be derived from the biblical poetry of Isaiah:

Be your sins like crimson,
They can turn snow-white. (1:18)

As Moses removed his shoes, something formerly done only by the high priests, more religious Jews observe the prohibition of wearing leather shoes and don sneakers instead. Unfortunately, *Yom Kippur* footwear issues have scaled up to Kafkaesque levels of absurdity in some ultra-Orthodox communities. Apparently, one rabbi ruled against the rubber slip-on shoe known by the brand name Crocs. In his eyes these nonleather shoes, while legally permissible, would not cause the wearer sufficient discomfort on this important day of penance. This is a perfect example of the kind of thinking that all modern Jewry, whether religious or irreligious, should avoid. It misses the point of religion, which is to ensure that we lead a decent, moral, ethical life.

For me, the most memorable part of this day is the Kol Nidre melody that marks the beginning of *Yom Kippur.* I have long struggled with boredom in synagogue services. I believe that the words we speak in prayer are important; that's why reciting Hebrew prayers that I don't understand often leaves me cold. But as author and journalist Abigail Pogrebin wrote in the online magazine *Tablet,* services don't need to become entertainment—their role should be "jarring us with illumination."

This is the case for me during the Kol Nidre prayer. Its words really don't have much meaning today. An Aramaic term, Kol Nidre means "All Vows," and the prayer is a dry, legalistic formula that asks God to release us from vows we have made to the divine. The prayer has a long and complicated history, the most popular interpretation, though not necessarily an accurate one, being that it provides an escape clause for those Jews who were forced to convert to Catholicism.

It is the melody that moves. Though I am not a mystic, I agree with the Jewish mystics who believed that the word-less voice, the *kol*, reflects something profound. In the case of Kol Nidre, the music used in the Ashkenazic Jewish tradition (I understand the Sephardic versions are equally profound) is for me the "voice" of *Yom Kippur.*

This piece, composed by Max Bruch, is inspired by two melodies found in a collection of Jewish liturgical music called MiSinai. The darkly radiant composition moves from pensive reflection to transcendent joy. As I listen, I find myself think-ing of the *conversos*, the secret Jews of Spain and Portugal who were forced to practice their Judaism furtively, their candles lit behind shuttered windows. For me, this image becomes a representative symbol of all the Jews who have held on to their traditions in face of dangerous, even murderous opposition. And when this music merges with the sun, red and lowering in the sky, along with my wild hope that through my honest reckoning of the past ten days the wounds I've inflicted on friends, family, and colleagues will somehow heal, the experi-ence is indescribable.

This feeling increases in intensity as I move through the day of *Yom Kippur.* It reaches its apex during the evening ser-vice, with its talk of heavenly gates swinging shut, sealing my fate, and the congregants' voices blending together in the haunting bars of Avinu Malkeinu ("Our Father, Our King"), an ancient, pleading prayer in which we ask for an end to pestilence, war, famine, hate, and oppression on earth. Then we hear the last, long blast of the shofar.

As you know by now, I don't believe in heavenly gates or a supreme being dwelling in a supernal realm whose job is to mete out punishments and rewards. Nonetheless, the symbols still speak if recast anew. For me, the closing of the heavenly gates is a reminder that life is short. At that moment, if I haven't done so already, I feel an urgency to get on with the all-important task of asking forgiveness from those I may have hurt. Similarly, as I listen to "Our Father, Our King," I hear a call to the most developed part of my consciousness, the ethical impulse, which when acted upon can contribute to the lessening of the world's woes.

HANUKKAH: THE FESTIVAL OF LIGHTS

My first *Hanukkah* memory has nothing to do with the story of the Maccabees, the lighting of candles, or even the taste of crispy potato latkes fried in oil to commemorate the miracle of lights. It was 1935 and I was around five years old, living in Montreal. When I opened a small envelope from Aunt Ann and Uncle Harry I found a five-dollar bill inside, with a note that said "*Hanukkah gelt*." I was bewildered. What did the holiday have to do with money?

It's been over seventy-five years since then, and while many changes have swept North American Jewry during that time, I fear my memory of *Hanukkah* isn't all that different from what many American children experience today. Because of the holiday's proximity to Christmas, in many homes the focus on *gelt* (Yiddish for money) has morphed from a few dollars to an outpouring of gifts. I suspect the presents provide many people with their first *Hanukkah* memory. And it's not just Jews who have begun to associate the holidays with gifts. All Americans are prone to turning to material possessions to celebrate winter holidays.

The societal pull that turns December into the "season of giving" is impossible to resist in much of the Diaspora. Even in my own life, I have fallen into that trap. Yet at *Hanukkah* we have a wonderful opportunity to give gifts of the nonmaterial kind. With its eight nights of celebration in the home, *Hanukkah* is a chance to engage with the small Jewish texts that we use in the most intimate of moments: blessings.

To me, the blessing is an opportunity to acknowledge that for which we are thankful. This *Hanukkah*, you might take your Judaism into your own hands and write a blessing for each child, one for each night of the eight-day candle lighting. Many topics are possible. You might tell them why you are grateful they are in your life and share your dreams for them. You might mention their special achievements and let them know how proud you are.

Many children might still prefer *gelt* at the moment. But more lasting is to say the words that connect your children to yourself, your family, and the Jewish people; to instill in them Jewish pride and a feeling of being safe and treasured. A blessing is a gift no one else can provide and one that will be among the greatest you can ever give.

Hanukkah, too, is a time to share the story of the Maccabees, which holds far more meaning than its usual retelling as a triumph over oppressors. While *Hanukkah* is not a major holiday, and receives only a brief nod in the Talmud, it contains some important ideas.

The central elements of the Maccabee story are contained in the apocryphal books I and II Maccabees. Around 175 BCE, a Greek king named Antiochus IV, ruler over a vast empire that included the land of Israel, was eager to consolidate his subjects under the banner of one belief. The Jews, like everyone else in the region, were ordered to bow low before the gods of the Greeks and assume Greek customs, including the eating of pork. Some Jews assimilated, embracing urbane Greek culture with its theaters and gymnasiums and its focus on science, philosophy, mathematics, and the arts. Other Jews stayed on the sidelines. Still others outwardly rebelled. This group of rebels became known as the Maccabees.

The Maccabees got their start in a small Jewish town called Modi'in. As related in Jewish apocryphal material, a Jewish high priest named Mattathias was asked to sacrifice a pig on a pagan altar set up for that purpose. When Mattathias refused, a Jewish villager came forward to take his place. Furious that a Jew would offer to take on the way of the Greeks, Mattathias killed the villager, and the Syrian officer too. At that point, Mattathias's five sons got into the act and killed all the other soldiers. Mattathias and his sons fled into the hills and caves of the Judean wilderness.

Mattathias died shortly thereafter—he was an old man, already in his eighties. But his son Judah, known by the nickname Maccabee, an Aramaic word meaning "hammer," led a guerrilla-style war for three years. Finally, the Maccabees were victorious and returned to Jerusalem to purify and rededicate the Temple.

They were aghast at what they saw. The city was in ruins and the Temple desecrated. The altar had been profaned with pig sacrifice and the gates burned down. The courtyards were thick with weeds. Idols remained standing. In their sorrow, the Maccabees tore their clothes, threw ashes on their heads, and fell facedown on the ground. But once they overcame their grief, they set to work repairing the Temple. They tore down the altar so that it would not stand as a monument to their shame, and put new stones in place. They dedicated the courtyards, made new utensils for worship, and brought the lamp stand, the altar of incense, and the table for the bread into the Temple. When all had been purified and rebuilt, they were ready to dedicate it anew.

Though the *Hanukkah* story is often presented as one of Jewish unity in the face of oppression, in its background is a civil war that pitted orthodoxy against adoption of the dominant Greek culture. Now, as we face the dangers both of Jewish zealotry and of widespread assimilation, I see *Hanukkah* as a clarion call for a liberal, questioning, Jewish education. In my view, *Hanukkah* is a perfect time for adults and more mature young Jews to engage in genuine discussion about the role of tradition. The more we know about our history, with its complexity and contradictions, its tragedies and triumphs, the richer our understanding becomes.

The story of the miracle of the oil, which is the reason behind the tradition of eating oily foods on *Hanukkah*, appears only in the Talmud, not in the Maccabee texts. As the story goes, when the Temple was rededicated, there was only enough olive oil to last for one day, which would not have been a sufficient length for celebration. Rather than wait for a new shipment of consecrated oil, the triumphant Jews lit the *menorah* anyway, and, miraculously, the oil lasted for eight days. One reason that has been suggested for this addition was that the rabbis of the Talmud were uncomfortable with drawing too much attention to the military victory and wanted to shift the focus instead to God's power.

For me, the resonance of the *Hanukkah* lights is not mainly in their reference to this long-ago tale, but in their symbolic glow during the darkest season of the year. *Hanukkah* is yet another opportunity to dedicate ourselves to the task, both as Jews and as human beings, of bringing light into the dark world. Judaism, ever hopeful, claims that this world can be redeemed. Like the *Hanukkah* candles, its light can grow brighter through one positive action after the other. There is no better way to bring light into the world than through education, both Jewish and secular. Rather than a handful of gold-wrapped chocolate coins, spinning tops, fried foods, and gaily wrapped packages, this is the real gift of the Festival of Lights.

PURIM: THE BOOK OF ESTHER

Purim is a joyful, often rollicking holiday that celebrates the saving of the Jewish people of Persia. The story is found in the book of Esther, which is also called the *Megillah*, a word that means "scroll." The word *Purim* means "lots" and refers to the lots that Haman, the story's villain, drew to help him decide the day when the Jews would be massacred. The holiday is celebrated in March, on the fourteenth day of the Hebrew month of Adar, the day our tradition assigns to the hanging of the evil Haman.

The narrative recounts the story of Esther, a young Jewish woman living in Persia with her uncle Mordecai in the fourth century BCE under King Ahasuerus, a man of tyrannical impulse. As the story has it, Ahasuerus orders his wife, Queen Vashti, to show her beauty before his male guests. When the queen refuses, the king, frustrated by her disobedience, seeks the counsel of his advisers. All of them speak against Vashti, fearing that if she goes unpunished, wives might get the idea that they too can refuse their husbands' orders. This in turn could cause great disruption in the kingdom. So King

Ahasuerus orders Vashti's execution. He then sets up a beauty pageant to find a new queen. Impressed with the dark-eyed Esther, he makes her his wife. She, fearful that her Jewishness will cause her trouble, conceals her true identity.

The evil star of this tale is Haman. A devious, power-mad adviser to the king, he is disgusted with Mordecai because he failed to kneel before him, so he plots to exterminate the Jewish people. In a chilling speech, similar in tone and content to the speeches of history's anti-Semites, he tells King Ahasuerus, "There is a certain people, scattered and dispersed among the other peoples in all the provinces of your realm, whose laws are different from those of any other people and who do not obey the king's laws; and it is not in Your Majesty's interest to tolerate them" (Esther 3:8).

The king is swayed by Haman's argument and gives him the green light to exterminate the Jews. But Mordecai is one step ahead. He convinces Esther to take up the matter with the king. This is no small thing, since appearing before the king without a summons could be punishable by death.

In preparation for her task, Esther first purifies her mind and body with a three-day fast. Then she approaches the king. King Ahasuerus reverses his decision and Haman gets his comeuppance at the end of the rope he had prepared for Mordecai. Even better? Mordecai is appointed prime minister. When he takes office, he passes a decree that allows Jews the right of self-defense.

Traditionally, Jews have not been drinkers, but there is a

dictum in the Talmud that orders us to become "fragrant with wine" on *Purim* (Megillah 7b). "Fragrant with wine" is not exactly stinking drunk, though that delicate description is contradicted by the idea that one should get so sauced that it's impossible to distinguish between the evil Haman and the blessed Mordecai. In the Talmud, where the sages put much emphasis on keen, clear minds, there is a good deal of discussion about what degree of intoxication is considered acceptable for *Purim*.

Another *Purim* custom is making noise to blot out the name of Haman, who is viewed as a manifestation of the dastardly nation Amalek, which according to the book of Exodus attacked the Israelites in the desert at their most vulnerable. In fact, there is a *midrash* that instructs Jews to engrave Amalek's name on two stones and then furiously bang them together. Eventually this would wear away the terrible name. Still another *Purim* custom is to write the name of Haman on the bottom of one's shoes and then stamp one's feet madly. The holiday also includes a recitation of the story of Esther, the wearing of carnival-like masks, the giving of charity, and copious amounts of food and drink.

It's too easy to see *Purim* as yet another example of the classic Jewish holiday formula: "They tried to kill us, we survived, let's eat!" *Purim*, however, is much more than a celebration of good over evil. Within the Jewish tradition, there is much speculation on the concept of "hiddenness" in the story. The name Esther means "hidden," and hiding her Jewishness was exactly what Esther did, in spite of pressure to reveal her ancestry. As a *midrash* explains, this enabled her to become queen, which in turn enabled her to save the Persian Jews. For religious Jews, the concept of hiddenness extends to the fact that the narrative does not mention God, with the exception of a vague reference to the fact that had Esther not succeeded in her mission, someone else would have come to the aid of the Jews. What we think of as luck or chance, according to this interpretation, is actually the work of a God who, though concealed, acts on behalf of the Jewish people.

From a secular perspective, I read the book of Esther as a story about the salvation of the Jewish people through the use of strategic thinking and bold actions. I also see *Purim* as a wonderful opportunity to study texts that tease the subtleties from the extremely complex issue of when subterfuge and falsehood might be necessary—an issue that, on deeper look, is at the heart of the book of Esther. The Torah doesn't mince words when it comes to the issues of deceit, clearly telling us not to bear false witness, steal, or lie, and to distance ourselves from corrupt matters, to cite a few of the injunctions meant to keep us honest. However, things are seldom so simple. Philosophers and religious leaders of all persuasions have weighed in on this issue. In his *Ethics*, Aristotle tells us that lying is never permissible, whereas in *The Republic*, Plato explains that some situations demand prevarication. The Talmud's discussions lean toward Plato, detailing cases when dishonesty might need to take precedence over truth-telling. To see the wisdom here, one only has to think of the two midwives in Exodus, Shifra and Puah, who used devious methods to thwart Pharaoh's plan to kill the Hebrew baby boys. In general, our sages rule that when honesty can lead to the harm of self or others, lying is permissible.

SUKKOT: THANKSGIVING AND REFLECTION

It's a shame that more Jews do not celebrate *Sukkot*, the weeklong autumn holiday that comes five days after *Yom Kippur*. With its festive mood, *Sukkot* stands in sharp contrast to the just-completed solemnity of the Day of Atonement. In fact, *Sukkot* is so joyful that it is sometimes referred to as the Season of Rejoicing.

The festival takes its name from the *sukkah*, the temporary structure built during the holiday under which it is customary to share meals, entertain, sleep, and rejoice. This shelter is tied to the harvest season of the ancient Israelites: To provide the farmers with respite from the sun, a hut was set up at the edges of fields. The *sukkah* is also connected with the temporary shelters built by the Israelites during their forty-year trek across the Sinai Desert.

Exacting rules define the construction of a *sukkah*. As tradition teaches, it must have a minimum of two and half walls and be large enough to hold a table. A *sukkah*'s roof needs to be made of natural elements through which one can see the stars.

In 2010, the *sukkah* was inspiration for an architectural design contest called Sukkah City, in which the winning entries were installed in New York City's Union Square Park. This contest was created by the writer and journalist Joshua Foer, whom I am proud to identify as an alumnus of the Bronfman Fellowships, along with Roger Bennet, the cofounder of the organization Reboot. This is a marvelous example of how Jewish traditions are being taken into the twenty-first century. The project attracted six hundred architects from over forty countries, and though they needed to follow traditional design restrictions, they were otherwise free to reimagine the three-thousand-year-old *sukkah*. The winning twelve booths were very different from the small, shabby tabernacles that housed the ancient Israelites, and none bore any resemblance to today's modest shacks decorated with children's drawings and colored lights that pop up in backyards and on rooftops. Yet all of them captured the symbolic meaning of the *sukkah*: homelessness, exodus, fragility, and our connection to the natural world.

While I unfortunately did not observe *Sukkot* when my children or grandchildren were growing up, I can now imagine how meaningful it might have been to celebrate the holiday together with children. I know that some of my most fascinating conversations have taken place during my efforts to Jewishly educate my grandchildren. I warmly remember those talks, especially those I had with one grandson, Aaron. Over regular lunches, we studied the Hebrew Bible together, working through it verse by verse.

Once, as we were just entering a restaurant, he expressed a deep concern about whether David, like Saul, would lose God's favor. I told him that was a pretty big subject, so we'd better sit down first. We then went on to have a great conversation that covered a lot of territory, including the scene in which David kills the armor-clad Philistine giant Goliath with a mere slingshot.

Of course great opportunities to teach and learn exist all the time, but in retrospect I see how these learning experiences might have been made even more memorable if they had taken place not only in the ordinary world, but also in the special world of the *sukkah*. I can picture us asking questions and searching for meaning beneath a slatted roof interlaced with green boughs, in the cool autumn air. In the quiet, sanctified space of the *sukkah*, we could have gone deeper into the story, exploring what it means to face a huge challenge, as David did. When do we ignore the rules and when do we follow them? What are some huge obstacles we confront in our own lives?

There is also a custom tied to *Sukkot* called *ushpizin* (Aramaic for "guests") in which important Jewish biblical figures are invited to the meal in the *sukkah*. Traditionally these figures have been male—Abraham, Isaac, Jacob, Joseph, and Moses—but today's practice also includes matriarchal figures like Ruth, Deborah, Sarah, Rebecca, and Esther. Aaron and I might have deepened our study by inviting Saul, David, and even Goliath to join us. After reading the story, we could have taken turns posing our questions to these three characters and imagining their answers. I am sure Aaron would have had a lot of questions!

Because of its link to harvest time, *Sukkot* also provides us with a chance to express thankfulness. If you have children, or when you do, you might draw up a list with them of all the people necessary to bring the beautiful foods to our table: those who cultivate the land, sow the seeds, and harvest the crops; and the chain of people—the packagers, deliverers, and distributors—needed to get the food to the table. A prayer of thanksgiving can be given to all these unknown individuals. Children could even write their own prayers to these unseen people.

I might take advantage of the slatted roof of the *sukkah*, especially on a clear, starry night, to call children's attention to the vast universe, because without an anthropomorphized God, we need something to humble us. As Spinoza pointed out, the starry sweep of sky perfectly meets that need. *Sukkot* is also a wonderful time to champion the cause of science, for as Einstein famously said, "Science without religion is lame, religion without science is blind." As we sit in the bough-decorated hut, we can discuss real miracles like photosynthesis with our children, helping them understand how a plant's leaves capture the sunlight and then turn it into sugar and drive the nutrients into its roots. *Sukkot*'s emphasis on nature could also call our attention to the degradation of our earth and food production, pointing out that if we permit global warming to go on unchecked, the earth will soon be unable to produce the food we need to survive.

For mature observers of the holiday, it can be a time to reflect on impermanence. The fragile *sukkah*, composed of wood, tin, boughs, sky, sunlight, moonlight, and starlight, is the very embodiment of the transitory nature of human life, an idea well expressed in this Jewish folktale of unknown origins:

One day, King Solomon summoned one of his trusted advisers. When the adviser arrived, Solomon explained to him that he'd be going on a mission in search of a special ring for *Sukkot*.

"What makes this ring so special?" the adviser asked.

"When a happy man looks at the ring, he becomes sad," said Solomon. "And when a sad man regards the ring, his sorrow turns to joy."

So the minister set off and scoured the land, searching for the mood-changing ring.

One night while walking in the poorest quarter of Jerusalem, he passed a tiny hole-in-the-wall store. He entered and discovered an old man polishing gemstones. "Have you ever heard of a ring that makes a happy wearer sad, and a sad wearer happy?" he asked.

The jeweler disappeared into the back of the store, and when he returned he held a velvet pouch in his hand. He unwound the tassel and pulled out a golden ring. After engraving something on the ring's interior, he handed the band to the surprised minister.

The minister, though relieved at finding the ring, was

nonetheless tired and anxious from his arduous search. But
when he gazed at the ring, his mood instantly lifted. Excitedly,
he hurried back to the palace and handed it to Solomon, who
was sitting on his throne, delighting in fruits, wine, and the
beauty of his dancing girls. But when Solomon regarded the
engraving on the band's interior, his smile immediately faded.
On the inside of the ring's band, the jeweler had inscribed,
"This too shall pass." In that moment, Solomon realized that
all his wisdom, wealth, and power were transitory things that
one day would turn to dust.

The message of impermanence can also be found in the
Hebrew Bible, in haunting lines like these:

> "Utter futility!" says the Teacher. "Utter futility! All is
> futile!" (Ecclesiastes 1:2)
> For we were born yesterday, and know nothing because our
> days on earth are a shadow. (Job 8:9)
> As for man, his days are like grass, he flourishes like a flower
> of the field. The wind blows over it and it is gone and its
> place remembers it no more. (Psalm 103:15–16)

This message of impermanence goes hand in hand with
Judaism's deep physicality. As a young man, I remember reading T. S. Eliot's poem "The Love Song of J. Alfred Prufrock."
At the end of the lyric, Prufrock is experiencing an anxious
moment, trying to decide whether or not he dare eat a peach.

I remember the teacher telling us that Prufrock's hesitation over the peach symbolized feelings of sexual inadequacy or discomfort.

In Judaism, I'm happy to share, "eating peaches" is kosher. The body and its joyous expressions are not considered sinful if they are treated with respect to self and others, an idea that expresses itself in laws of moral purity in marriage. Deprivation of the body and its many joys is not a Jewish concept. Part of this, I believe, comes from Judaism's love affair with the physical world.

Still, we must be cognizant of the fact that things of a physical nature do not last. In traditional Judaism, we leave the earth wrapped in a white shroud with no pockets, symbolizing that we cannot take anything with us. This idea can be part of *Sukkot* as well. As we sit in our fragile *sukkah*, surrounded by the fruits of harvest, the rich profusion of the earth before the winter comes, we can remind ourselves that power, fame, and riches all fade away. These are great things that have their place, and I've been extremely privileged to have had them all. But the love we share with our family and fellow travelers during our very brief sojourn on earth far surpasses anything we can own. As I write this at the age of eighty-four and a half, I know it to be profoundly true. We should remind ourselves of the importance of spending time with those we love, because as I can attest, the years pass very quickly, and unless we make the time, we will never find it.

SIMCHAT TORAH: REJOICING IN THE TORAH

Simchat Torah begins two days after *Sukkot* ends. The name of the holiday translates as "rejoicing in the Torah," and indeed it is a time of great joy. The holiday marks the completion of the Torah reading cycle and the beginning of the next one. Customarily, the Torah scroll is rewound, and recitations include the final verses of Deuteronomy and the opening lines of Genesis. The purpose of this is to show the continuity of the Torah; it is a book that has no end and no beginning.

During the observance of *Simchat Torah*, the Torah is passed from one person to the next. People even dance with it and cradle it as if it were a precious child. Children carry small paper sacks that are filled with candy to suggest the sweetness of learning. The dancing procession often moves throughout the synagogue or bursts into the streets.

It was this celebration, when I witnessed it in within the repressive environment of Moscow in the 1970s, that piqued my curiosity and helped inspire me to learn about Judaism. *Simchat Torah* is a perfect time for making a commitment or recommitment to Jewish study and learning. The idea here— that Jewish learning is a dance of the mind, and one that should never end—is one I now wholeheartedly embrace.

TU B'SHVAT: BIRTHDAY
OF THE TREES

When I was about twenty-one and my brother Charles was nineteen, we took a road trip across the United States. As young Canadians, we were eager for an adventure through the American West. We experienced the stunning vistas of Utah, the Grand Canyon in Arizona, and the great redwoods of Yosemite National Park in California. As I looked on those majestic trees, I began thinking of trees in general and their many gifts: They shield us from sun and keep our soil from eroding; they generate the oxygen that allows us to live; they provide us with wood, paper, fire, fuel, medicine, and food. Thinking about all this, I was filled with a sense of awe.

The Jewish holiday of *Tu B'Shvat*, literally translated as "the fifteenth day of [the Hebrew month of] Shvat," is thought of as the Birthday of the Trees. It is a perfect time to express our wonder and appreciation for the natural world and an opportunity to remind ourselves that we are stewards of the planet we share.

Like many Jewish holidays, *Tu B'Shvat* is rooted in an agricultural event, in this case the prohibition against harvesting the fruit of a tree until its third year. The reasons behind this were practical: A too-early harvest of dates or almonds could harm the maturing trees. Another mandate required Hebrew farmers to give a tenth of their harvest as gifts to the poor as well as to members of the priestly class. To ensure that these commandments were properly observed, a specific date, the fifteenth of Shvat, was selected. Like a tax date, this helped farmers know when the tithing was due.

Farther down the corridor of Jewish history, these agricultural traditions were given a new meaning by the sixteenth-century mystic Rabbi Isaac Luria, who was based in the city of Tsfat (also known as Safed). Inspired by the idea that the Torah itself is often called the Tree of Life, Luria and his disciples saw a chance to infuse these agriculturally based commandments with spiritual significance. Taking their cue from the Passover Seder, Luria and his disciples created the concept of a joyous meal involving four cups of wine—white, pink, light red, and dark red, each color reflecting a different season—along with fruits, nuts, roots, and seeds set up on tables draped with white cloths. Fragrant water and sweet-burning candles added to the festivities.

During the Seder, the fruits eaten fell into three categories: those with inedible shells (such as oranges and pomegranates), those with inedible pits (dates, olives, and so on), and those that are completely edible (such as figs and raisins). The sages ascribed symbolic meanings to the various kinds of fruits and tied the budding of spring with the renewal and redemption of the Jewish people.

Over time, the holiday took on a more secular meaning when the early Zionists recast it as a way of strengthening the connection between the Jews and their ancient land. Today, in both Israel and the Diaspora, it is gaining favor as a holiday that elevates environmental consciousness. Given our dying coral reefs and overfished seas, our denuded forests and burning rain forests, our melting ice caps and landfills packed with nonbiodegradable items, this awareness has never been more vital or significant than it is today. This is why I recommend making *Tu B'Shvat* a more prominent holiday in the Jewish calendar of festivals.

Some have claimed that the tie between Judaism and today's ecological concerns is contrived, often citing the lines in Genesis as evidence of Judaism's alienation from nature:

And God said, "Let us make man in our image, after our likeness. They shall rule the fish of the sea, the birds of the sky, the cattle, the whole earth, and all creeping things that creep on earth." (Genesis 1:26)

But Judaism has always been closely tied to the protection of the natural world. According to recent biblical scholarship, the word that is usually translated as "dominion" in the Genesis text in fact has a meaning that is closer to "stewardship." Throughout Jewish sources, one can find principles that emphasize the human connection to and responsibility for the natural world.

One of those is *bal tashkhit*, which translates as "you will not destroy." The purpose of this principle is to protect the land, animals, and plants from senseless destruction. The commandments relating to this idea prohibit the cutting down of fruit trees during wars. In fact, Maimonides went so far as to suggest that those who needlessly destroyed fruit trees, whether in war or peacetime, should be flogged.

Today this idea could be expanded to prohibitions against the destruction of rain forests and old-growth forests. Those who exploit our natural resources could be "flogged" with heavy penalties. Expressions in the Talmud also warn against water pollution and damage caused by noise and smoke, as well as the waste of lamp oil, ripping up useful clothes, and chopping up good furniture for firewood. I speculate that our sages would be in full support of noise ordinances and banning smoking in public places.

There are also many laws regarding the ethical treatment of animals, both wild and domestic. It is notable that the Jews created a whole set of laws, condensed into the concept of *tza'ar ba'alei chayim*, whose sole purpose is to minimize the suffering of animals. These laws expressed themselves in numerous ways, from kosher laws governing the ways animals are slaughtered for food to a ban against hunting as a sport. More than this, *Shabbat* was also a resting period for animals, as noted in Exodus, and Jews were forbidden to muzzle their animals while threshing. Nor could animals of different species be yoked together as their different sizes and strengths would create undue hardship when plowing.

Compassionate identification with and for animals wasn't a given in the ancient world, though it is commonplace today. My strongest sense of connection with an animal was with a horse I once had named Hudson. One night Hudson, a superb jumper, escaped from his stable. As he walked up the road, he crossed a cattle guard, and his leg slipped between two cement bars, breaking it. He appeared to be in great pain, and died during the night. The sorrow I felt for Hudson continues to this day.

Judaism does not mandate vegetarianism, but its rulings attempt to minimize the suffering of animals that are used and consumed by people. One of these rulings appears in Deuteronomy:

> If, along the road, you chance upon a bird's nest, in any tree or on the ground, with fledglings or eggs and the mother sitting over the fledglings or on the eggs, do not take the mother together with her young. Let the mother go, and take only the young, in order that you may fare well and have a long life. (22:6–7)

Maimonides comments on this passage, saying the injunction gives us a chance to practice compassion. In his *Guide of the Perplexed* he writes:

> As far as pain is concerned, there is no real distinction between the pain of humans and the pain of animals, because the love and compassion of the mother for her young is not reasoned intellectually, but has only to do with emotions and instincts, which are found among animals no less than among human beings. (3:48)

Though things have improved, domestic and wild animals are still the victims of human neglect and cruelty. *Tu B'Shvat* could provide us with an opportunity to focus our attention on urgent environmental and animal rights issues. From awareness-raising Seders to hands-on involvement or financial support of groups such as the Coalition on Environment and Jewish Life (COEJL), Hazon, Jewcology, Teva Learning Center, and the Wilderness Torah, we can use this holiday to help our badly suffering planet.

There are many wonderful *midrashim* that convey the interconnections between human beings and the natural world. Here are two that might be told at a *Tu B'Shvat* Seder:

A man named Choni approaches an elderly man planting a carob tree. "How long will it take for that tree to grow?" he asks. When the man replies seventy years, Choni scornfully laughs. "Seventy years?" he says. "What makes you think you'll be here to harvest the fruit?" The old man replies, "When I came into this world, it had many carob trees. As my parents and forebears planted carob trees for me, I now plant them for my children" (Taanit 23a).

And another: A group of people are sitting in a boat. All of a sudden, one member of the group takes out a tool and begins hacking a hole beneath his seat. "What are you doing!" his terrified fellow passengers cry out. He answers, "Making a hole. But it's no business of yours. It's under my seat!" (Leviticus Rabbah 4:6).

These simple stories, and so many like them, remind us

that we must never forget that what one person does or doesn't do has profound, even life-and-death consequences for other people and creatures, both those alive now and those to come. And while I am immensely proud that our people and tradition developed and implemented an environmental ethos long before our planet was in such a degraded state, we can't rest on our laurels. Now more than ever we need to be stewards of our environment, and *Tu B'Shvat* is a perfect way to encourage Jewish involvement.

SHAVUOT: RECEIVING THE TORAH

Like *Sukkot* and *Tu B'Shvat*, the joyous spring holiday of *Shavuot* has roots in the Jewish people's ancient agricultural cycle. The holiday, which celebrates the harvest, the book of Ruth, and the giving of the Torah, has intriguing origins. In the Bible, instructions regarding the celebration of *Shavuot* are not entirely clear. First, when is *Shavuot* to be observed? The text does not specify exact dates: "You must count until the day after the seventh week—fifty days; then you shall bring an offering of new grain to the Lord" (Leviticus 23:16). We are not told which Sabbath is being referred to. The beginning of the chapter provides dates for Passover, but the connection between the Passover verses and the section about *Shavuot* is somewhat tenuous.

Several other questions remain unanswered: "You shall bring from your settlements two loaves of bread as an elevation offering; each shall be made of two-tenths of a measure of choice flour, baked after leavening, as first fruits to the Lord" (Leviticus 23:17). What is being celebrated or commemorated? What is the purpose and theme of this holiday? Other holidays have a clear historical theme and commemorate a significant event in the past. This festival, however, seems to be detached from any historical context.

The holiday that evolved from these rather obscure and incomplete verses is a terrific example of the way Judaism uses a skeletal biblical text as a starting point for creating an immense body of work in which imagination and commitment to values dictate the direction its development will take. A rich, extensive tradition evolved from these few verses—a tradition that supports crucial themes in Judaism and brilliantly solves a number of problems.

First, an agricultural holiday without a tie-in to a historical event could be demoralizing when the land itself was lost. With the exile of the Jews in the sixth century BCE by the Babylonian conquest, and the resulting diaspora, Jews would no longer be farming in the Promised Land. By inserting a celebration of the giving of the Torah, this difficulty was solved.

Including the book of Ruth in observances of the holiday adds yet another dimension. The iconic image from Ruth is of the two women, Ruth and her mother-in-law, Naomi, gleaning the leftover wheat that Jewish law requires farmers to leave for the poor. The book of Ruth is also notable for its treatment of the theme of intermarriage. Ruth is originally from the tribe of Moav, but she marries an Israelite, and when he dies she remains loyal and loving toward Naomi. *Shavuot* thus, through the book of Ruth, brings women to the forefront, and serves as a reminder that acceptance of foreigners and converts, as well as care for the poor, are essential to Jewish life and thought.

But the most important aspect of the holiday is the receiving of the Torah. There is an interesting ritual leading up to this holiday known as *Sefirat HaOmer*, translated as "the Counting of the Sheaves" or, more commonly, "the Counting of the *Omer*." During this forty-nine-day period between Passover and *Shavuot*, we count up, perhaps reflecting the idea that receiving the laws at Mount Sinai is the apex of the Exodus story. Without these ethical and moral imperatives, the liberation from Egypt would have no meaning. It could also suggest that this is a time for "elevating" or improving our moral and spiritual selves; during these days, we can meditate on how to be more courageous, more disciplined, and, above all, more loving human beings.

During the holiday, the book of Ruth is read in synagogue, along with medieval poems called *piyyutim*. It is traditional to eat dairy products on *Shavuot*, a custom for which there are many explanations, including connections to ancient sacrificial offerings, to the dietary laws regarding separation of milk and meat, and to a line from the Song of Songs, "honey and milk are under your tongue," which is interpreted by the rabbis of the Talmud as a comparison to the sweetness of Torah (4:11).

Celebrations of *Shavuot* may also include a *Tikkun Leil Shavuot*, when participants stay up all night to study Torah. This tradition, which originated among medieval mystics, has been adapted into communal nights of Jewish learning. For both secular and religious Jews, these events, which may include poetry, song, food, and theater, are a vibrant and authentic connection to Jewish culture.

TISHA B'AV: DAY OF MOURNING

Traditionally, the somber day of *Tisha B'Av* mourns the destruction of the First and Second Temples, which occurred in 586 BCE and 70 CE, both during the month of Av. Gradually, however, the holiday expanded to include all the catastrophic events in Jewish history, from the expulsion of the Jews from Spain in 1492 through the Holocaust. The holiday often includes fasting and reading from the book of Lamentations. *Tisha B'Av* is an opportunity to deepen our understanding of painful episodes in Jewish history and to observe a day of mourning for these tragedies and for those that unfold today.

In looking to traditional sources on *Tisha B'Av*, one idea worth pondering is the Talmudic concept that "baseless hatred" (*sinat chinam*) caused the destruction of the Second Temple. During this period, the Jews were divided into various groups with great ideological differences. These differences escalated into a civil war. The sages of the Talmud do not blame the victim but identify as a cause of the catastrophe the irrational, destructive quality in human nature.

Tisha B'Av is the holiday that immediately precedes the month of Elul, when we observe *Rosh Hashanah* and *Yom Kippur* and engage in the process of self-reflection and asking forgiveness. In its exploration of notions of suffering and responsibility, *Tisha B'Av* leads up to this period in a deeply philosophical way, completing the cycle of the year.

YOM HASHOAH (HOLOCAUST REMEMBRANCE DAY) AND *YOM HA'ATZMAUT* (ISRAEL INDEPENDENCE DAY)

Two modern holidays have arisen to commemorate the tragedy of the Holocaust and the triumph of the state of Israel. Both are observed in the Jewish community across denominations, and both have great significance for secular Jews.

Yom Hashoah

Yom Hashoah, inaugurated in Israel in 1953, is the shorter form of *Yom Hashoah Ve-Hagevurah*, which translates into "the Day of Remembrance of the Holocaust and Heroism." This solemn day arrives one week after Passover and coincides with the anniversary of the Warsaw Ghetto Uprising of 1943. While it is less commonly observed in North America, the Israeli Knesset has decreed it to be a day to be remembered.

Starting in the 1960s, *Yom Hashoah* has been marked with sirens blaring throughout the country, their piercing cry causing the whole nation of Israel to come to a stop. Pedestrians stop walking, vehicles stop moving, and people pause all activity to participate in two minutes of silent reflection. Additionally, no entertainment takes place on this day, and radio and television programs are devoted to subjects concerning this tragic topic, including the stories of survivors.

After the Holocaust, the phrase "Never Again" became the determined vow not only of the survivors themselves but also of fellow Jews throughout the world. This profound assertion of self-protection was passed on to their children through efforts to educate them about the Holocaust and to document its history. Today, the phrase has been adopted by the world at large—particularly younger Jews—as a rallying cry to end all genocide.

Among American Jews, there is an increasing generational rift in the way the phrase is used. Older Jews like myself who came of age when the atrocities of the Holocaust were at their most palpable and immediate remember the first cry, "Never Again," as the anguished response of the Jewish people. While all genocide is pure evil, the Holocaust, in its scope and scale, is unique on the world stage. Those who lived through its atrocities saw the world stand aside as Jewish men, women, and children perished in concentration camps, their hopes, dreams, and lives suffocated in poisonous gas, their bodies burnt to ashes in the ovens' terrible flames. With this tragedy seared into their consciousness, and in too many cases tattooed on their skins, they responded with the resolve to fight anti-Semitism worldwide and to ensure Jewish cultural continuity.

Because of this, my generation of Jews is somewhat reluctant to embrace the younger Jewish interpretation of "Never Again" to mean all genocide, while younger generations seem unwilling to be aligned with an attitude that privileges Jewish suffering. Having grown up in a country where anti-Semitism is no longer a part of daily life, they are less concerned with the struggle for Jewish survival than with a search for joy and meaning in Judaism. Those who embrace the second feel less commitment to the vigilance on behalf of Jews that the first vow demands. They resist the call for self-protection, and instead focus on the Jewish value of justice and the pursuit of *tikkun olam*, the repair of the world.

While I admire this confidence and openness, the embrace of the second "Never Again" has also come at the cost of the first. The younger generation tends to gloss over the real dangers that Jews face today, which include rising anti-Semitism in Europe and the Middle East.

On Holocaust Remembrance Day, Jews of all ages and generations might come together to remember this painful history and to understand the vigilance needed to ensure that it never happens again. At the same time, we could use this event as a time to explore the question: Who are we as Jews and as human beings if we look away from the suffering of others?

In the end, "Never Again" does not need to be either/or. We should keep the memory of this heinous crime against the Jews alive to remind ourselves of the Jewish value of taking responsibility both for our own community and for any other community in need.

But because I believe, in the Jewish way, that hope should trump fear, we should also recall the words of Prime Minister Levi Eshkol, who said in his Holocaust Day Address in 1965:

> Holocaust Memorial Day falls between the ancient Festival of Freedom and the modern day of Israel's Independence. The annals of our people are enfolded between these two events. With our exodus from the Egyptian bondage, we own our ancient freedom; now, with our ascent from the depths of the Holocaust, we live once again as an independent nation.

Yom Ha'atzmaut (Israel Independence Day)

Israel, whatever her flaws and blemishes, is the antidote to the Holocaust; she is the fabled phoenix that quite literally arose from the ashes. Israel Independence Day commemorates the founding of the state of Israel on May 14, 1948. Like Independence Day in the United States, Israel's Independence Day is celebrated with dancing, singing, picnics, and family outings. Along with these festive events, the army showcases technological innovations and the "Israel Prize" is awarded to individual Israelis, recognizing their accomplishments in a range of fields, from science to the arts.

However, since 1967, the world—including many Jews—is not always in the mood to celebrate our Jewish state. More than any other nation on earth, Israel has suffered from a barrage of criticism, some of it legitimate, some of it a veiled form of anti-Semitism. I am not of the mind that says "my Israel right or wrong." I have been both a supporter and a critic of Israel for as long as I can remember. But there are two types of criticism: One is supportive and constructive; the other is angry and vituperative. And when it comes to the delegitimization of Israel's right to exist that we have seen over the past several years, I would say that the criticism tilts toward anti-Semitism.

I also have little patience for the cultural relativism that plagues much of the opinions one hears about Israel, especially on many American and European college campuses with their endless petitions to arrest Israeli leaders and boycott Israeli products. Strangely, these same voices are silent when it comes to buying iPhones from China, a country with human rights abuses that far outstrip Israel's record. And they almost always pay scant attention to the atrocities perpetrated by nations other than Israel and the United States.

But even within Israel, depending on where one falls on the political spectrum, feelings about Israel's Independence Day vary widely. Some members of the left-wing parties, post-1967, see it as an unappealing ethnocentricity. On the opposite end, many right-wing groups take an overly militaristic stand, casting Israel as a victim among the world's nations, and disparage any hope of peace between Israel and Palestine. Even worse, some extremist religious parties do not celebrate the founding of the secular state in 1948 at all, preferring to wait for the fulfillment of some ill-begotten dream of the annexation of the West Bank.

As we've already explored, Judaism thrives on questions. The many dissenting voices in our community should not be pushed out, but engaged. As in the Talmudic tradition of dialectic reasoning, we can show that we care and are connected to each other by rigorous inquiry, not blind advocacy and belief. In that spirit, I would encourage all Jews to use this holiday not only as a time to celebrate Israel's many accomplishments, but also as an opportunity to explore the many views surrounding this seemingly intractable conflict, particularly in light of our relationships with the Palestinians, for it is here that the rubber of Jewish ethics meets the moral road.

On Israeli Independence Day I would like to see the institution of *Yom Ha'atzmaut* Circles in synagogues and communities where Jews of multiple views could come together to discuss books that put forth different ideas on Israel's situation, from Alan Dershowitz's *The Case for Israel* to David Grossman's novel *To the End of the Land*. In these circles we could also raise and explore central questions: What is our responsibility to the Palestinians? Can Israel be a democratic state and a Jewish state? What Jewish values should be sacrosanct in Israel? What is the connection between Israelis and Diaspora Jews? How can we ensure equal rights for all the citizens of Israel? The Arab population within Israel has much larger families than the Israelis (with the exception of the religious Jews). Eventually this will lead to Jews being a minority in their own country. What will happen to the concept of Israeli democracy when the majority of citizens are not Jewish?

I can see no better way of celebrating the miracle of Israel than in the time-honored Jewish value of questioning.

CHAPTER 8

Freedom Revealed

The idea that it's possible to move from slavery to freedom and from darkness to light and from despair to hope—that is the greatest Jewish story ever told.

—Rabbi Sharon Brous, from a PBS interview

WHEN I WALKED INTO THE HOUSE THROUGH THE back door one day as a young man, I was shocked to see my mother in the kitchen. To put it mildly, this was not one of her favorite places. When I asked her why she was there, a look of panic crossed her face. "Now that Grandma's gone," she explained, "I have to make the *haroset*." Sensing her culinary discomfort, I volunteered to take over. With a look of vast relief, she fled the scene.

Guided by the memory of my grandmother's *haroset*—the sweet, chunky, fruity mixture that symbolizes the mortar the Hebrew slaves used to build Egypt's real estate—I chopped up apples and walnuts and added raisins. I mixed them together then added a couple of spoonfuls of honey and a generous splash of port wine.

During the Seder, my *haroset* received wild compliments all around. "Who made this?" my father asked, clearly pleased. Without hesitation, my mother told him I had done so. When asked for my secret, I proudly answered, "Good port."

I don't think it's a stretch to suggest that my hands-on involvement, combined with the warm, welcoming embrace of my efforts, contributes to my love of Passover, the holiday most deeply embedded in the Jewish consciousness. Though its earliest origins may be as a spring festival, and to be sure, many elements of the spring agricultural celebration remain, those elements gradually evolved into the eight-day holiday we celebrate today during the month of April.

In celebrating Passover, we fulfill the injunction, "Remember this day, on which you went free from Egypt, the house of bondage, how the Lord freed you from it with a mighty hand" (Exodus 13:3). The theme of a journey from subjugation to freedom is at the heart of the Passover story, and there is a strong emphasis on repeating the liberation story every year and to each generation:

This day shall be to you one of remembrance: you shall celebrate it as a festival to the Lord throughout the ages; you shall celebrate it as an institution for all time. Seven days you shall eat unleavened bread; on the very first day you shall remove leaven from your houses, for whoever eats leavened bread from the first day to the seventh day, that person shall be cut off from Israel. (Exodus 12:14–15)

This stern direction to remember our own story of liberation and keep it alive across generations lifts it into universal resonance. The Exodus from Egypt is not to be seen as a one-time historical occurrence with a beginning and an end: oppression, struggle, victory. It is not only those slaves, but all slaves, that concern us; not only that struggle, but all struggles. Each generation must learn anew how to overcome the wrongs of the world; the job will never be done. Children will not be born into a perfect world created for them by their parents. They can only continue to hold the torch, and their parents' role is to teach them how to carry on the fight for justice.

That is why the Passover ritual is central to Judaism. It is so crucial that whoever does not keep it, the Bible tells us, will be cast out and will no longer be considered a part of Israel. In other words, this is the premise of Judaism: If you are to be a part of the people, you must struggle to maintain or realize freedom all your life.

Central to the celebration of Passover is the Seder, a special feast that evokes the memory of our own servitude and reminds us that it is our duty to tend to the weak, alleviate the discomfort of the poor, and fight for the rights of the disenfranchised.

The Seder is guided by a special booklet known as the Hagaddah. The Hagaddah, which began thousands of years ago as a spare text of about 450 words, evolved over the centuries into a dense and at times bewildering compilation of rituals, blessings, songs, stories, and commentary. This greatly embellished text became known as the "traditional" Hagaddah. In recent years it has been rewritten by thousands of writers, both professional and amateur, each with their own take or theme. Writing a Hagaddah, as I did myself, is an excellent opportunity for cultural Jews to create a book that complements their interests and spiritual orientation.

In the sections below, I explore the symbols and traditions that the Haggadah traditionally contains and offer my own interpretations. I encourage all to approach their observance of Passover with a creative, questioning approach that makes it relevant to their own lives.

THE PASSOVER STORY

Passover is rooted in the biblical story of the Exodus, which was created over a long span of time by many authors. While the story's historicity has not been proven, it is not generally regarded as pure invention either. Like the rest of the Bible, the book of Exodus is probably a mix of history, myth, and legend. However, in the end, trying to determine or explain what is historically true and what is the result of human imagination misses the point. The story's message remains an astonishing one, particularly in light of the time when it was created.

Until this narrative, no story took the freeing of slaves as its central theme. No story focused so insistently on the idea that society must be ruled by moral laws. And while other ethical guidelines in the tradition preceded the Ten Commandments—notably Hammurabi's Code and the Hebrew Bible's Noahide Laws—the Exodus narrative is unique, as it asserts that the condition of freedom is inextricably linked to the practice of moral responsibilities.

The Passover story raises many ethical questions, and a Seder meal often includes long and spirited discussion and debate. For example, one might ask, when reading about God's smiting of the firstborn of the Egyptians and the drowning of the hordes that came after the people of Israel, if it was right for all Egyptians to be punished for their leader's recalcitrance. The story, which we are commanded to remember and repeat, is meant to raise questions and to force us to seek answers.

The story really begins four hundred years before the Exodus, with a Hebrew named Joseph who lives in the land of Egypt. Joseph, originally from Canaan, had been sold into slavery by his jealous brothers. Because of his extraordinary ability to interpret dreams, he has won his freedom and risen to prominence in Egypt.

After reconciling with his brothers, Joseph brings his extended family from Canaan and settles them in Goshen, one of Egypt's most fertile districts. Because of his brilliant rationing strategies, Egypt is spared the worst of a famine ravaging the region. As a result, the Egyptians revere Joseph and his tribe—the Hebrews, or Israelites. During these years, the children of Israel increase until the land is filled with them.

Everything changes when a new king arises in Egypt. This new ruler worries that the Israelites might join with Egypt's enemies should war break out. He makes their lives bitter with hard bondage and forces them to build the treasure cities of Egypt.

Still, the Israelites swell in number. So Pharaoh turns to population control: He assigns two Hebrew midwives, Shifra and Puah, the task of killing every firstborn Hebrew male baby at birth. Secretly the midwives thwart the order, explaining that the Hebrew mothers gave birth before the two arrived to assist. The furious Pharaoh then orders his soldiers to find every firstborn Hebrew boy and cast him into the Nile.

During this time, a woman named Jocheved gives birth to a son. For three months she conceals the baby, but when she realizes she can no longer hide him from the Egyptians who are looking for Hebrew boys to drown in the Nile, she builds a tiny ark and sets her baby among the reeds. Enter Pharaoh's daughter, who, hearing Moses' cry as he floats among the reeds at the Nile's banks, says, "This must be a Hebrew child." Yet she does not betray him. Instead, she speaks with Moses' sister, Miriam, who waits nearby and who arranges for Moses' own mother to suckle him.

As the story goes, years pass, and Moses becomes a prince of Egypt. Yet he often feels a strange longing, especially when watching the Hebrews toiling under the scorching sun as they build the treasure cities of Ramses and Pithom. One day, as an overseer whips an elderly Hebrew slave, Moses can no longer suppress his rage. He commands the overseer to stop. When the slave driver ignores his order, Moses kills him and buries the body in the sand. One of Pharaoh's men witnesses the killing. When Pharaoh learns what Moses has done, he orders that he be killed.

Moses, however, has escaped to a place called Midian, where he marries a young woman named Zipporah, the daughter of Jethro. The couple have two sons, and Moses remains with his family in Midian for many years.

One day, while Moses is tending Jethro's flock at the foot of Mount Horeb, also known as Sinai, he sees a bush shimmering with fire, though its leaves and branches are not consumed. Suddenly he hears a booming, otherworldly voice that commands him to remove his sandals. The voice identifies itself as the God of Moses' forebears, Abraham, Isaac, and Jacob, and instructs him to go down to Egypt and bring his people to Mount Horeb. He promises then to take them to Canaan, a large and lovely land.

Moses argues with God, explaining that he lacks the speaking ability and authority to be a leader. Eventually God wins him over, assuring him that his brother, Aaron, will assist him with speaking, and provides him with the power to perform several miracles.

With his wife, Zipporah, and sons, Moses returns to Egypt. In the desert, he meets Aaron, who has been instructed by

God to appear. They agree that Aaron will do the talking and perform the miracles God has described. When Moses and Aaron share the liberation plan with the tribes' elders, they all bow down, relieved to learn that God has heard their desperate pleas.

But when Moses and Aaron ask Pharaoh to allow the Israelites to make a short trip into the desert to worship their God, Pharaoh refuses. He knows nothing of this God, and believes a good day of work will be lost. So instead of granting the request, he orders his slave masters to increase the labors of the Hebrews. The slaves blame Moses and Aaron for their added misery.

On their next visit to Pharaoh, Moses instructs Aaron to perform the miracle of turning a rod into a snake. Pharaoh counters by having his magicians do the same. As soon as this happens, Aaron's rod swallows the smaller snakes. Pharaoh is unimpressed.

God then commands Moses to put forth his request again while Pharaoh is bathing in the Nile. If Pharaoh denies the request, Aaron is to hold his rod over the Nile, and all the water in Egypt, even that in the water jugs, will turn into blood. Soon blood streams throughout all of Egypt and there is no drinking water anywhere. But Pharaoh remains obstinate, especially when it appears that his own magicians may have reversed the spell.

God then visits other plagues on Egypt. Each is more severe than the last: frog infestation, gnats and lice, flies or wild animals, diseased livestock, boils, thunder and hail, locusts, darkness. Before the final plague, the death of Egyptian firstborn, God tells Moses to instruct all the Israelites to mark their doors with lamb's blood, so that the Angel of Death will pass over the houses. It is from this part of the story that the name Passover derives. At last, Pharaoh relents and allows the Hebrew slaves to go.

The Israelites depart hastily without even waiting for the bread in their kneading troughs to rise. They begin their long walk to freedom. By day they are guided by a whirling pillar of cloud, by night a brilliant column of fire.

Back in Egypt, Pharaoh's heart hardens again, as do those of his courtiers. He commands his generals to bring back the fleeing Hebrews, and the Egyptian troops speed after the escaped slaves. Soon the Israelites, who are camped on the shore of the Sea of Reeds, hear the rumble of approaching chariot wheels. They cry out in doubt and fear. It would have been better to remain as slaves in Egypt, they shout, and they accuse Moses of leading them to death, not to freedom.

Moses calls out to the people and tells them not to fear. When he stretches out his rod, an easterly wind blows. The wind stirs up the water, heaping it into two growing walls, with a wide, dry path in between. According to a *midrash*, with Egypt's militia bearing down fast, an Israelite named Nahshon breaks from the crowd and boldly steps onto the path. The Israelites rush behind him as he crosses through the divided sea and leads the people to the other side.

In the biblical account, we learn that when the Egyptians follow behind the Israelites, Moses causes the waves to roll back into place, and the Egyptians disappear and their cries are heard no more. With that, Moses' sister, Miriam, rushes to the shore and leads the women in a joyous song of liberation.

After their cruel forty-nine-day journey through scorching heat and howling winds, suffering thirst and hunger, and attacks from the Amalekites, Moses leads the exhausted Israelites to the plain near Mount Sinai, where they make camp. The mountain itself is ablaze in light and engulfed in the loud sounds of trumpets. Leaving his terrified people in camp, Moses ascends the mountain, where the story's author tells us that God gives him the words that become known as the Ten Commandments, here in slightly shortened form:

I am the Lord your God who brought you out of Egypt…. You shall have no other gods besides Me.

You shall not make for yourself a sculptured image, or any likeness of what is in the heavens above, or on the earth below, or in the waters under the earth. You shall not bow down to them or serve them….

You shall not swear falsely by the name of the Lord your God….

Remember the Sabbath day and keep it holy….

Honor your father and your mother….

You shall not murder.

You shall not commit adultery.

You shall not steal.

You shall not bear false witness against your neighbor.

You shall not covet your neighbor's house: you shall not
   covet your neighbor's wife, or his male or female slave,
   or his ox or his ass or anything that is your neighbor's.
   (Exodus 20:2–17)

When Moses returns, he finds that in his absence, the
restive former slaves have built a golden calf to worship. In
a fury, Moses smashes the tablets of the law, but, moved by
something—a sense of mission? compassion?—he creates a
second set for the disobedient slaves. At the end of the journey
we learn that Moses himself is not allowed into the Promised
Land, though his people, who have been wandering in the desert for forty years, cross over the Jordan River.

The many themes of this story—the idea that hope dwells
in the darkest place, that tyranny can be overcome, and
that freedom and responsibility are inextricably linked—are
reflected in the special foods we eat and rituals we perform
at the Seder. While many of the customs are associated with
theistic beliefs, they easily lend themselves to secular interpretations. All share the purpose of bringing alive the story, of
reminding us that though we once experienced the degradation of slavery, we now enjoy the dignity of free people. And
while each of these things has accrued traditional meanings
over thousands of years, all should feel free to come up with

original ideas. Learn the past and invent the future. Passover is an excellent opportunity to exercise this creativity.

Candle Lighting

There is of course a practical reason for candles' centrality in Jewish practice. Prior to electricity they, along with oil lamps, were the only source of light.

Nevertheless, candles retain profound symbolism in Judaism. For the traditional Jew, they represent the soul, derived from the line in the book of Proverbs, "The soul of man is the candle of God" (20:27). As a cultural Jew, I am reminded by the candles used at the Passover Seder of the importance of keeping the fragile flame of freedom alive in the world.

Elijah's Cup

The prophet Elijah represents a redeemed world free of racism, slavery, cruelty, poverty, and greed. As has been the custom for centuries, during the Seder a door is traditionally opened to welcome Elijah, and a cup of wine for him is ready on the table. The wine in his decorated cup symbolizes the joyful world that Jews are commanded to build.

When my wife and I began working on a Hagaddah together, she asked why the door was opened for Elijah at the end of the meal, not at the beginning. The interpretations for why we open the door have evolved from the Middle Ages, when it was commonly believed that we did this to ask for God's protection, to now, when it is seen as welcoming a holy presence at the table. But I interpret the open door as a symbol of the mandate to welcome all visitors to the Seder table, and to be generous in sharing the bounty of our festive meal.

To that end, in the Hagaddah we wrote, my wife and I made the decision to invite Elijah in at the beginning of our meal. As the Jewish people, we should prioritize welcoming those who are not included. We are all inheritors of a beautiful and wondrous religion, and we must be generous in embracing the unaffiliated and disenfranchised. To open the door at the beginning of the meal, not at the end, is to signify our intention that no one should be left out as we celebrate this holiday of freedom.

Elijah's symbolic presence also reminds us that "Egypt" is still with us: Oppression remains a scourge, in the United States and around the world. As long as people are suffering beyond our doors, we can never be truly free.

Matzo

The story of Exodus tells us that when the Israelites left Egypt, they had no time to prepare leavened bread: "And they baked unleavened cakes of the dough that they had taken out of Egypt, for it was not leavened, since they had been driven out of Egypt and could not delay; nor had they prepared any provisions for themselves" (Exodus 12:39). Matzo, the unleavened bread eaten in the desert, has become the central

symbol of freedom, while *hametz*, or food containing a leavening agent, is forbidden so that we can remember that slavery
was left behind.

But the message behind the eating of matzo is more than a
tribute to freedom.

In the Bible, Passover is referred to as "the Feast of the
Unleavened Bread," or *Hag Hamatzot* (Leviticus 23:6). The
powerful message that comes to us is that freedom is not about
physical comfort and luxuries. It is about choice and responsibility. The same act has very different meanings depending
on our reasons for it.

In addition, the matzo, which we are required to eat only
during the first two nights of Passover (for the remainder of
the holiday we need only avoid *hametz*), reminds us of all those
who do not have enough to eat and who live in dire poverty
and destitution. That is why, in the traditional Hagaddah,
the reference to the "bread of affliction" that begins the ceremony is followed immediately by the ideology behind the
eating of matzo: "Let all who are hungry enter and eat, let all
who are in need come and join the Passover with us. This year
we are slaves, next year may all be free."

Throughout the Seder, the matzo is used in various ways.
One Seder ritual called *yachatz* breaks a piece of matzo that is
between two others. Over time, this custom has accrued multiple meanings. Some believe it represents the parting of the
sea; for others it is the breaking apart of slavery's shackles. It
also reminds us of the two great events in our ancestors' quest

for freedom: the escape from physical bondage in Egypt, and the receiving of the Ten Commandments at Sinai.

The custom of hiding a piece of matzo, the *afikomen* (Greek for "dessert"), originally referred to a Talmudic prohibition against eating dessert after the Seder meal. However, over time it evolved so that during the Seder it may be discovered by a child in return for a small gift. The anticipation of finding the hidden matzo helps keep children awake during the meal.

Zeroa

The *zeroa* is a roasted lamb shank bone, though other animal shank bones are also sanctioned. In vegetarian Seders, the traditional replacement is a roasted beet.

This symbolic food commemorates the Paschal Lamb and the sacrifices made at the Temple, and lambs are also universally associated with spring. It also recalls the lamb's blood the Israelites placed on their doorposts in the Passover story so they would be spared the tenth plague, the death of the firstborn. Like the other foods on the Seder plate, the shank bone is not meant to be holy in any way, and that is why replacing it with another symbolic food has become common.

Karpas

The origin of the word *karpas*, the vegetable we dip in salt water at the Seder, is a mystery. Is it related to the Greek word for fruit of the harvest, *karpos*, or to *karafs*, the Persian word for parsley? One *midrash* points out that when the letters are rearranged, the word means "hard labor," an idea that might suggest that joy and sorrow are inseparable.

On the Seder plate, the *karpas* greens, usually parsley, signify the coming of spring. One of Passover's names is *Hag Ha-Aviv*, the spring holiday, and the greens remind us of the natural beauty and bounty of crops during this time.

During the Seder ritual, we dip the greens in salted water, which symbolizes the tears of the oppressed slaves. This act asks us to empathize with the suffering of our ancestors and with all people who have experienced persecution. Along with the beauty of spring, we experience the taste.

Maror and *Haroset*

The Torah commands us to commemorate the deliverance from slavery by eating the Paschal sacrifice "with unleavened bread and with bitter herbs" (Exodus 12:8). The word used is *maror*, the Hebrew word for "bitter." The Talmud specified that the bitter herb had to be a root vegetable, but the terms used for recommended vegetables are obscure to us.

The bitter herbs, usually ground horseradish, have come to be seen as a symbol of the bitterness and misery of the Israelites under slavery. Since the Seder is supposed to be an active reenactment or personal immersion in the story, we eat a bitter food to help us personally imagine the suffering of a slave.

Because Jewish tradition attempts to balance the bitter with the sweet, we include, along with the *maror*, the sweet mixture called *haroset*. This can be made of any fruits and nuts. One tradition is to use foods mentioned in the biblical Song of Songs, but recipes for *haroset* abound, and different countries have their own customs. The standard Ashkenazi (Eastern European) recipe calls for apples, cinnamon, nuts, and wine, but many recipes include pomegranates, raisins, pears, dates, figs, and so on.

Like all the symbolic foods of Passover, the *haroset* has a paradoxical significance. It represents both the suffering of bondage (mortar) and the sweetness of freedom. It reminds us that our hard-won freedom is always fragile, and that there is still oppression in our present-day world. The sweetness of the *haroset* does not mask the bitterness of the *maror*, and vice versa. Both have significance, and both are part of our journey.

Baytzah

The roasted egg, or *baytzah*, on the Seder plate, is a symbol replete with meaning. The egg is meant to recall the Temple sacrifices and the fertility of the land. Most centrally, its round shape reminds us of the cycle of life and of the natural process of death and rebirth that spring exemplifies. The renewal of spring brings hope and regeneration. The past may be full of regrets and mistakes, but a new start and a second chance is always possible.

The Four Children

This traditional reading describes four types of children who respond to the traditions of the Seder: one wise, one wicked, one simple, and one who does not know how to ask questions. I see this passage as containing a wonderful lesson. Each of the children—rebellious, agreeable, silent, or bewildered—participates in the act of questioning. When I think of the four children, I am keenly aware of the responsibility—in fact, the necessity—of constantly interrogating our tradition and attempting to understand our place in it.

Miriam's Cup

Despite the extraordinary role women play in the Exodus story, they are mentioned only once in the traditional Hagaddah, and in a very minimal way: Miriam makes a brief appearance in a song in the night of the Seder. There are many explanations for the absence of women in the traditional Hagaddah, one being Hellenistic influences on the Jews. The Seder itself, in fact, is modeled after the Greek symposium in which scholars gathered to eat and drink multiple glasses of wine as they discussed intellectual ideas with male colleagues. These symposiums did not include women, who were generally relegated to the private, not public, spheres. Yet without the work of five stellar women—Shifra and Puah, Jocheved, Miriam, and Pharaoh's daughter—the Exodus would never have happened. These admirable women did not wait for a God to save them. They took destiny into their own hands and fixed what needed fixing. And they were resolute, unwavering in their commitment to solving the problem. Above all, they risked their own lives to save the life of a small child and the Jewish people.

Inspired by several *midrashim*, many Seder tables now include an item known as Miriam's Cup. Various rituals can be developed around Miriam's Cup. For some, it represents the miraculous well that traveled with the Israelites and supplied water as they trekked through the wilderness. Without it, the Israelites would have died of thirst. There is poetry in this, as Miriam's name means "sea," and when she died, the well disappeared. In *The Bronfman Haggadah*, I suggest that we use this as a time to remember a special woman in our life.

Ten Drops of Wine

There is a beautiful *midrash* associated with the parting of the Sea of Reeds. Although the biblical account describes the Hebrew singing at the destruction of the Egyptians, the *midrash* tells another story. In this story, the angels are cheering as the waters roll back into place, plunging the Egyptians to their deaths. But when the angels request permission to rejoice, God grows angry and admonishes them: "The works of my hands are drowning in the sea, and you want to rejoice?" (Megillah 10b). I don't believe in angels, but this story imaginatively makes an important point: While Jewish tradition sanctions the right to self-defense, it instructs us to always celebrate life, not death—even the death of our enemies.

This concept is expressed in the traditional Passover custom of casting drops of wine from our glasses onto our plates. With a finger, we each remove ten drops—one for each of the plagues. In doing so, we express our aversion to the punishments meted out to the Egyptians during our ancestors' deliverance from slavery. As long as others suffer—even our enemies—our own joy, symbolized by the wine in our glasses, is lessened.

The Four Questions

The Four Questions are recited, usually by the youngest child who can manage them, near the start of the Passover Seder. At the heart of the Four Questions is really one question—"Why is this night different from all other nights?"—that expands into four examples.

The Hagaddah evolved over the centuries, and the questions were not always the same ones we are accustomed to hearing today. In addition, sometimes the child would ask the questions but the father would answer them. Today the child asks and answers the questions in a familiar liturgical tune.

Raising questions is typical of the Jewish approach to interpretation, and the chanting of the Four Questions sets the tone for the Seder. It also gives children a central role, immediately engaging them and marking the Seder as a family event. In a sense the youngest members are the stars of the show. The

Seder is about them and for them. It is they who must learn about Jewish history, texts, and traditions so they can bring them into the future. In the grand narrative of the Exodus, reexperienced through the Seder ritual, we find the universal resonance and power that make me confident our tradition will endure.

CHAPTER 9

A Lesson in Leadership

The Bible is literature, not dogma.
   —George Santayana, introduction to *The Ethics of Spinoza*

For lack of vision a people lose restraint,
But happy is he who heeds instruction.
                                    —Proverbs 29:18

IN JEWISH TRADITION, THE TORAH IS DIVIDED INTO
fifty-four portions, or *parashot*, the plural of *parashah*. Every
week a portion is read, chanted, or sung in the synagogue on
Saturday morning.

Parashah readings are often coupled with an oral commentary by one of the participants. These commentaries draw
their ideas from a creative interpretation of a word, phrase,
theme, juxtaposition, character, or any other related topic that
emerges from the biblical text. The beauty of this tradition is
that the participant does not need to be a scholar or possess

a warehouse of Jewish knowledge. *Parashot* can also be read at home with the family, and this is a practice I wholly support. In fact, I've always been a proponent of making *parashah* study a part of *Shabbat*, and it can just as easily become part of the Passover Seder. Seder guests could each interpret the *Parashat B'shalach*, which tells the Exodus story, through a lens of personal interest.

The story's grand narrative of oppression giving way to freedom might be viewed in multiple ways. One person, for example, might see it as a blueprint for personal transformation, casting its characters into roles that represent a psychological process. Another might approach the story from a feminist viewpoint, focusing on the women whose contributions ensured the survival of the Jewish people. Still another might understand it as a metaphor for the artistic process or as a road map for organizational change.

My fascination with the Exodus narrative, and with Moses in particular, springs from my interest in leadership, especially the kind of leadership needed to fulfill a moral purpose or vision. I am aware that many excellent business books have addressed the principles and practices of leadership embedded in the Exodus story, but most focus on Moses the manager. I am less interested in this than in Moses the man who, flawed as he was, executed brilliant strategies that ultimately transformed much of the world. These principles are also relevant to everyday leadership, from parenting to day-to-day responsibilities at work.

You might be wondering why I've chosen to conclude this book with a brief analysis of the leadership principles embedded in the Exodus narrative. My reasons are several. First, I wanted to highlight the influence of Moses and the Exodus story in general, given their unique place in the Jewish tradition. As summarized by writer, activist, and Holocaust survivor Elie Wiesel in his book *Messengers of God*:

> It is not surprising that [Moses] occupies a special place in Jewish tradition. His passion for social justice, his struggle for national liberation, his triumphs and disappointments, his poetic inspiration, his gifts as a strategist and his organizational genius, his complex relationship with God and His people, his requirements and promises, his condemnations and blessings, his bursts of anger, his silences, his efforts to reconcile the law with compassion, authority with integrity—no individual, ever, anywhere accomplished so much for so many people in so many different domains. His influence is boundless, it reverberates beyond time.

I find it a shame that the curriculum of today's typical secular school, unlike that of former times, generally excludes the Bible. The Exodus narrative in particular deserves attention, because Moses and his story have informed so many American institutions. The Bibles of the Pilgrims were illuminated with images of Moses, and our Founding Fathers, steeped in the Hebrew Bible, chose to engrave Moses' words, "Proclaim

Liberty throughout all the Land unto all the Inhabitants Thereof," on what eventually became known as the Liberty Bell. The story even inspired the artist who created the Statue of Liberty. The rays circling her head are meant to reflect the light that supposedly emanated from Moses' face when he received the Ten Commandments. And of course the story is the inspiration behind many spiritual masterpieces: "Turn Back Pharaoh's Army," "Oh, Freedom," "I Am Bound for the Promised Land," and the most famous song of them all, "Go Down, Moses."

Because of this powerful emphasis on freedom, Moses and the Exodus have been embraced as touchstones for groups rebelling against oppressive powers. While some of those applications are less commonly known, and less appealing— as in the case of white southerners applying the moniker "Pharaoh" to Abraham Lincoln—other appropriations are familiar, such as Dr. Martin Luther King's famous use of Exodus imagery. Of his many references to Moses, his final speech, "I've Been to the Mountaintop," delivered on April 3, 1968, at the Mason Temple Church of God in Memphis, is almost eerie, as it was delivered twenty-four hours before a bullet took his life:

And then I got to Memphis. And some began to say the threats, or talk about the threats that were out. What would happen to me from some of our sick white brothers? Well,

I don't know what will happen now. We've got some difficult days ahead. But it doesn't really matter with me now. Because I've been to the mountaintop. And I don't mind. Like anybody, I would like to live a long life; longevity has its place. But I'm not concerned about that now. I just want to do God's will. And He's allowed me to go up to the mountain. And I've looked over. And I've seen the Promised Land. I may not get there with you. But I want you to know tonight, that we, as a people, will get to the Promised Land. So I'm happy, tonight. I'm not worried about anything. I'm not fearing any man.

That mountaintop was of course Mount Nebo, where Moses saw the vision of the Promised Land. Dr. Martin Luther King, like Moses, led his people on a heroic struggle, though he himself died before he was allowed into the Promised Land, which to King would have been the ultimate success of the civil rights movement.

In addition, I wanted to demonstrate how a Jewish text—in this case the Exodus story—yields both practical and philosophical wisdom. And finally, I am hoping that after reading this book you may be inspired to develop your own programs, projects, or institutions that address the central aims of Judaism—to advance the cause of justice and to repair our battered world. If so, these principles can be useful.

Let's turn to the story now.

TAKE A STAND

One day, when Moses had grown up, he went out to his kinsfolk and witnessed their labors. He saw an Egyptian beating a Hebrew, one of his kinsmen. He turned this way and that and, seeing no one about, he struck down the Egyptian and hid him in the sand. (Exodus 2:11–12)

The leaving of the known world, literally and figuratively, is the first step in any journey, and the story of Moses is no exception. At this point, Moses may or may not be aware that he is a Hebrew. In fact, as Freud speculates in his book *Moses and Monotheism*, a case might be made for Moses' being an Egyptian who was motivated by the idea of monotheism that some believe Akhenaten, the Pharaoh of Egypt, briefly dabbled with. But it does not matter whether Moses leaves his place at the palace with a small band of Hebrew slaves to establish a new religion, or whether he is motivated to do so by his identification with the slaves. Either way, he is leaving the place of false identity and separating himself from identities he can no longer own.

This is the first required step in leadership: Leaders must take a stand on something they strongly believe in and be ready to leave the known or comfortable world. True leaders must find a way to be connected to every segment of society; they must become part of the world and not limit themselves to a small circle that does not challenge them and never will.

What happens next is quite shocking. Moses, a prince of Egypt, who may or may not know about his Hebrew roots, feels allegiance to a slave. This is completely removed from the natural order of things. To fully appreciate the enormity of his action, we need to understand how inconceivable it would be for a boy raised in the Pharaoh's palace to side with a slave. Growing up in the palace, he would have learned that slavery is the natural order of things. And yet some part of him—the part I call "godly"—knows that beating a defenseless human being is wrong.

In a society that drowned the babies of slaves, it is not difficult to deduce what "beating" might be. As history teaches, in any society that sanctions slavery, the abuse of slaves knows few limits, for there are always those who will use the opportunity to exert power in its most extreme and brutal forms. The King James Version of the Bible translates the beating that Moses observes as "smiting," a particularly cruel form of striking. Thus the beating Moses witnessed could mean hitting to the point of near death, and Moses' response may not be as impulsive and irrational as it first appears.

This is not meant to condone vigilante justice. Rather, we can see this story as a metaphor for the extent to which Moses was ready to separate himself from the oppressor, the extent to which he was unwilling to tolerate injustice, and the extent to which he was willing to take matters into his own hands, even at the risk of his own safety.

This action might also suggest that there is no ambiguity

in Moses if we read the killing of the overseer as a symbolic "killing" of his old or false self as an Egyptian prince. He has heard the call and is ready to take it on. This is fundamental to all leaders. Once they hear the call to duty, they must be clear on their stance and not equivocate.

DISMISS REJECTION

When he went out the next day, he found two Hebrews fighting; so he said to the offender, "Why do you strike your fellow?" He retorted, "Who made you chief and ruler over us? Do you mean to kill me as you killed the Egyptian?" Moses was frightened, and thought, Then the matter is known! When Pharoah learned of the matter, he sought to kill Moses; but Moses fled from Pharoah. He arrived in the land of Midian, and sat down beside a well.

Now the priest of Midian had seven daughters. They came to draw water, and filled the troughs to water their father's flock; but shepherds came and drove them off. Moses rose to their defense, and he watered their flock. (Exodus 2:13–17)

As it turns out, the person who witnessed Moses burying the Egyptian is a Hebrew. The next day, when Moses intervenes in a quarrel between two slaves, he is met with contempt. We would expect these Hebrews, who clearly knew about Moses' killing of the overseer, to show gratitude. Instead, they challenge him, foreshadowing the challenges and complaints that will plague him once the quest for the Promised Land begins in earnest.

Moses could have given up at this point. He could have decided that his identification with the slaves had been misplaced. Here he was, risking his life to protect a slave, and instead of gratitude he is reviled and, even worse, betrayed.

Yet Moses does not become bitter and he does not turn a blind eye to the women at the well. His insistence on standing up for the oppressed—a theme that runs through the whole Exodus narrative—continues to guide him.

EXPAND YOUR WORLD

When they returned to their father Reuel, he said, "How is it that you have come back so soon today?" They answered, "An Egyptian rescued us from the shepherds; he even drew water for us and watered the flock." He said to his daughters, "Where is he then? Why did you leave the man? Ask him in to break bread." Moses consented to stay with the man, and he gave Moses his daughter Zipporah as wife. She bore him a son whom he named Gershom, for he said, "I have been a stranger in a foreign land." (Exodus 2:18–22)

This time, Moses is rewarded for his courage and integrity. In return, he receives not only a home, but a wife and child. For Moses, his stay in Midian with Reuel (Jethro) and his family is a transitional period. He has left his old identity, but has not yet fully embraced his new self. His old identity has been thrown off, but his new one is not yet known.

This period can be a very enriching time in a person's life, as it provides opportunities to expand one's knowledge and skills. This is exactly what happens with Moses in Midian. He learns a new language. He learns new customs and takes on new roles—husband, shepherd, and father—all of which provide him with the vital skills he will need for the journey ahead. It is not a coincidence that the old order, symbolic of Moses' former self, disappears while he is in Midian. He is now ready to receive the vision that will define his quest.

DEFINE YOUR VISION

Now Moses, tending the flock of his father-in-law Jethro, the priest of Midian, drove the flock into the wilderness, and came to Horeb, the mountain of God. An angel of the LORD appeared to him in a blazing fire out of a bush. He gazed, and there was a bush all aflame, yet the bush was not consumed. Moses said, "I must turn aside to look at this marvelous sight; why doesn't the bush burn up?" When the LORD saw that he had turned aside to look, God called to him out of the bush: "Moses! Moses!" He answered, "Here I am." And He said, "Do not come closer. Remove your sandals from your feet, for the place on which you stand is holy ground. I am," He said, "the God of your father, the God of Abraham, the God of Isaac, and the God of Jacob." And Moses hid his face, for he was afraid to look at God. (Exodus 3:1–6)

Up to this point, Moses has only had a feeling about what is right; however, he does not have a vision. A vision is essential because it is both a blueprint for building and a well for inspiration. And though visions continue to develop over time, they must be firmly in place at the start of a quest.

It is worth noting that the vision comes to Moses after he has been educated. He has learned the way of politics, power, arts, and philosophy from the Egyptian court, and in Midian he garners practical and human skills. He has also distanced himself from the tumult and noise that are a part of any power center. The very quiet, more spacious reality of the desert prepares him to receive the voice emanating from the burning bush, an image I read as a symbol of the highest part of our consciousness.

The story has moved quickly up to now. In swift strokes we have learned the facts of Moses' early years. The story slows down, taking on an almost chantlike quality:

And the LORD continued, "I have marked well the plight of My people in Egypt and have heeded their outcry because of their taskmasters; yes, I am mindful of their sufferings. I have come down to rescue them from the Egyptians and to bring them out of that land to a good and spacious land, a land flowing with milk and honey, the region of the Hittites, the Amorites, the Perizzites, the Hivites, and the Jebusites. Now the cry of the Israelites has reached Me; moreover, I have seen how the Egyptians oppress them." (Exodus 3:7–9)

This repetition drives home the affliction, the sorrows, and the brutal oppression of Moses' people. At the same time, the use of the luscious phrase "a land flowing with milk and honey" imbues the vision with hope and promise. When unfolding a vision to followers, a leader cannot simply focus on freedom from all that is negative in their lives, which in the case of Moses would be liberation from slavery. The vision must also have a positive element, because people do not merely want to leave something bad; they want to know where they are going, they want to know that their future will be brighter and better. This is a part of human nature, and it is essential for a leader to communicate this to his followers.

BE PRAGMATIC

"They will listen to you; then you shall go with the elders of Israel to the king of Egypt and you shall say to him, 'The LORD, the God of the Hebrews, manifested Himself to us. Now therefore, let us go a distance of three days into the wilderness to sacrifice to the LORD our God.' Yet I know that the king of Egypt will let you go only because of a greater might. So I will stretch out My hand and smite Egypt with various wonders which I will work upon them; after that he shall let you go. And I will dispose the Egyptians favorably toward this people, so that when you go, you will not go away empty-handed. Each woman shall borrow from her neighbor and the lodger in her house objects of silver and gold, and clothing, and you shall put these on your sons and daughters, thus stripping the Egyptians." (Exodus 3:18–22)

In the midst of the story's sweeping statements about slavery, and amid its evocation of a land overflowing with milk and honey, the focus suddenly shifts to the silver and gold of the Egyptians. This kind of pragmatism is needed in every great undertaking. A leader with a grandiose vision most likely will not succeed in realizing his goals, for there will always be basic, fundamental needs to attend to. Moses wisely takes care of this side of things, not as an act of revenge, but as a necessary step for the survival of his people.

It is also worth noticing that the women are given a crucial task. In doing this, Moses communicates that everyone will be involved in the struggle toward freedom. Women are not mere appendages who follow where the men lead as wives and daughters. They must ensure that the slaves leave Egypt with valuables. From these two things we learn that a good leader must be practical as well as visionary, and that no one must feel that they are not important and are excluded from the great events that are taking place.

FOCUS ON STRENGTHS

But Moses spoke up and said, "What if they do not believe me and do not listen to me, but say, 'The LORD did not appear to you'?" The LORD said to him, "What is that in your hand?" And he replied, "A rod." He said, "Cast it on the ground." He cast it on the ground and it became a snake; and Moses recoiled from it. Then the LORD said to Moses, "Put out your hand and grasp it by the tail"—he put out his hand and seized it, and it became a rod in his hand—"that they may believe that the LORD, the God of their fathers, the God of Abraham, the God of Isaac, and the God of Jacob, did appear to you."

The LORD said to him further, "Put your hand into your bosom." He put his hand into his bosom; and when he took it out, his hand was encrusted with snowy scales! And He said, "Put your hand back into your bosom."—He put his hand back into his bosom; and when he took it out of his bosom, there it was again like the rest of his body.—"And if they are not convinced by both these signs and still do not heed you, take some water from the Nile and pour it on the dry ground, and it—the water you take from the Nile— will turn to blood on the dry ground." (Exodus 4:1–9)

Once we understand the symbol of the serpent or cobra in ancient Egypt, the point of this image becomes clear. Serpents or cobras were signs of power in ancient Egypt. Pharaoh's headdress featured a cobra at its center, known as the Uraeus. It conveyed legitimacy to the ruler, and the Pharaoh was recognized only when wearing the headdress. Thus, later in the story, when Moses' serpent consumes the magicians' snakes, the suggestion is that Pharaoh's rule will be overcome.

The staff itself can be construed as a symbol of support, and as I see it, a strong vision is like a "staff": It sustains us and bolsters us when we are up against powerful forces. Similarly, it is like medicine: It can help cure the disease or problems we are up against. Pharaoh's rule is like the leprosy the white scales on Moses' arm suggests: cruel, insidious, and disfiguring.

From a leadership perspective, I see these three "miracles" as symbols for the kind of transformation that can happen when we believe in our cause. Without this belief—which is the kind of magic available to us all—our chance for success is slim. As Ralph Waldo Emerson wrote in his treatise on self-reliance, "Trust thyself: every heart vibrates to that iron string." In the case of Moses, that "iron string" is a shepherd's staff.

Paradoxically, we need to admit to our fears of failure. Moses is full of hesitation about taking up the reins, and comes up with a list of reasons why he is not fit for the leadership role God is assigning, protesting that no one will believe him; that he is not eloquent; and, worst of all, that the people will want to kill him.

This is the voice of self-doubt, of fear, of wanting to hide and to avoid the road that is set before us. At this stage, Moses is a reluctant hero, though he ultimately yields to his fate and prepares to return to Egypt.

Some commentators read Moses' initial response as a sign of humility and modesty. I see it as arising from self-doubt. Every leader must overcome self-doubt, though not by burying it under false bravado. And while Moses will need to move beyond his shortcomings, it is normal, natural, and right to give voice to them at the start.

FIND ALLIES/DELEGATE AUTHORITY

The LORD said to Aaron, "Go to meet Moses in the wilderness." He went and met him at the mountain of God, and he kissed him. Moses told Aaron about all the things that the LORD had committed to him and went and assembled all the elders of the Israelites. Aaron repeated all the words that the LORD had spoken to Moses, and he performed the signs in the sight of the people. (Exodus 4:27–30)

A vision must be followed by an impulse to act. And to act, one needs a plan. The first step, therefore, is to create a structure that can accommodate strategies and plans; in other words, it is crucial to be organized. This includes finding allies and delegating authority. In order to achieve their goals, leaders must understand that cooperation and structural organization are essential. Moses cannot embark on his mission alone and unaided. He needs co-leaders and allies who can help him.

Once the vision of his mission takes hold of him, Moses begins building partnerships and alliances. The strongest alliance is with his brother, Aaron. He also includes, to a lesser degree, his sister, Miriam. The emphasis here is on the importance in leadership of building bonds with others that do not comprise rivalry or power struggles. The importance of finding the right partner, the right second in command or assistant deputy, the person—or handful of people—who can be trusted with your life, is critical to effective leadership.

It is also interesting to note that while Aaron is clearly second in command, Moses understands he must work with him as a colleague and an equal. If he tries to exert power over Aaron, the mission can easily be put in jeopardy. The harmony of this partnership is reflected more than fifty times throughout the text, as Moses' and Aaron's names are linked together at moments of action and decision-making; for example: "The Lord said to Moses and Aaron" (7:8); "Then the Pharaoh summoned Moses and Aaron" (8:4).

The harmonious relationship between the two brothers also serves as a model to the people, showing that true leadership, unlike dictatorial or tyrannical systems, involves sharing and mutual respect. Miriam, Moses' sister, is also part of the leadership team.

The biblical account tells us that in some ways Moses could

be remote from the people he is leading and at times even contemptuous. His closeness is to God, or, in a secular reading, to the task he is seeking to fulfill. Miriam, on the other hand, works closely with the people, though, like Moses, she is far from perfect. In fact, when Miriam and Aaron question Moses' leadership because of his marriage to an Ethiopian woman, saying, "Has the LORD spoken only through Moses? Has He not spoken through us as well?," God punishes Miriam with leprosy, turning her white as snow (Numbers 12:2 and 12:10). According to one *midrash*, Aaron was spared this punishment because it would have interfered with his duties as high priest.

However, whatever their human failings, Moses, Aaron, and Miriam taken together form a powerful triumvirate of leadership, each one contributing to the bringing of the people to the Promised Land.

TEST THE WATERS

Afterward Moses and Aaron went and said to Pharaoh, "Thus says the LORD, the God of Israel: Let My people go that they may celebrate a festival for me in the wilderness." But Pharaoh said, "Who is the LORD that I should heed Him and let Israel go? I do not know the LORD, nor will I let Israel go." They answered, "The God of the Hebrews has manifested Himself to us. Let us go, we pray, a distance of three days into the wilderness to sacrifice to the LORD our God, lest He strike us with pestilence or sword." But the king of Egypt said to them, "Moses and Aaron, why do you distract the people from their tasks? Get to your labors!" And Pharaoh continued, "The people of the land are already so numerous, and you would have them cease from their labors!"

That same day Pharaoh charged the taskmasters and foremen of the people, saying, "You shall no longer provide the people with straw for making bricks as heretofore; let them go gather straw for themselves. But impose upon them the same quota of bricks as they have been making heretofore; do not reduce it, for they are shirkers; that is why they cry, 'Let us go and sacrifice to our God!'" (Exodus 5:1–8)

Moses and Aaron begin with a relatively limited request when they approach Pharaoh. They ask if the people can go and hold a feast to their God in the wilderness. There is much to recommend starting small, because the responses you receive can yield a great deal of information about whom you are dealing with. Not surprisingly, however, Moses quickly learns that he is up against an intractable foe. Pharaoh is a megalomaniac who is cruel and obsessed with power. In fact, Moses' request makes him even more sadistic: The slaves are no longer given straw, and because they spend so much time searching for straw, they cannot meet their brick quota. They are then beaten for not meeting the quota, and accused of being idle.

Moses' initial request to Pharaoh might be thought of as gradualism, a political belief that change should be brought about in incremental steps rather than large, disruptive uprisings or revolutions.

As Moses learns, the gradualist approach will not work. Compromise and step-by-step solutions are not going to be effective with Pharaoh. Making matters worse, the lives of the slaves deteriorate; their tasks are increased and made more difficult. He begins to lose heart. Where are all the promises that God made? Where is the power Moses drew upon when he saw the burning bush? It seems to disintegrate all at once.

HOLD FAST TO THE VISION

Then the LORD said to Moses, "You shall soon see what I will do to Pharaoh: he will let them go because of a greater might; indeed, because of a greater might he shall drive them from his land." (Exodus 6:1)

As God reminds Moses, he must move past setbacks and have faith in his vision, which is encapsulated in a strong, concise message—a message that has resonated throughout history: Let my people go. We can only understand the immensity of this request when we consider that the entire economy of Egypt depended on slave labor. Such an economic model, however, is morally repugnant and ultimately unsustainable, for humans are not and will never be objects or machines, and humanity cannot tolerate extremes of oppression.

REPEAT THE MISSION

God spoke to Moses and said to him, "I am the LORD. I appeared to Abraham, Isaac, and Jacob as El Shaddai, but I did not make myself known to them by My name. I also established My covenant with them, to give them the land of Canaan, the land in which they lived as sojourners. I have now heard the moaning of the Israelites because the Egyptians are holding them in bondage, and I have remembered My covenant. Say, therefore, to the Israelite people: I am the LORD. I will free you from the labors of the Egyptians and deliver you from their bondage. I will redeem you with an outstretched arm and through extraordinary chastisements. And I will take you to be My people, and I will be your God. And you shall know that I, the LORD, am your God who freed you from the labors of the Egyptians. I will bring you into the land which I swore to give to Abraham, Isaac, and Jacob, and I will give it to you for a possession. I am the LORD." But when Moses told this to the Israelites, they would not listen to Moses, their spirits crushed by cruel bondage. (Exodus 6:2–9)

One literary aspect of the story of Moses that we cannot fail to notice is the use of repetition. Certain phrases appear again and again. What is the purpose of this repetition? How many times does Moses need to hear these words? And how many times do we need to hear them?

The repetition is not accidental. Leaders must recognize that it takes time for people to grasp and internalize new information and new concepts, particularly when they are too dejected or demoralized to hear the message at first. This was the case with the Hebrews.

Faith is not an entity that, once found, remains with the finder forever. Faith is something that needs to be worked at. This is why leaders must repeat their message until it sinks in. They must not be discouraged if their message is not understood at first—how can it be when it is all so new? Instead, they must persist in conveying that message until it becomes second nature to all those around them.

The repetition of the message is also a way to remind ourselves that what we are doing is important; that we cannot be defeated; that transformation is possible. And that is why the message of Moses' mission is repeated again and again.

The poetry of the language is also an integral part of the narrative. Poems and songs speak to our emotions and go deep into our hearts. Inspiration is, at least at the early stages, more important than information.

We also see that in chapters 7, 8, and 9 of Exodus, Moses repeats his request to Pharaoh in the exact same language: Let my people go. Why is this refrain used again and again? Why does Moses not vary the message? By repeating the same phrase multiple times, Moses makes it clear that there is only one moral imperative in this situation. There is only one way of looking at oppression and tyranny, only one interpretation, only one truth. There can be no compromise.

This is why Moses' words to Pharaoh are so plain, concise, brief, and to the point. Slavery and oppression are unacceptable. Moses is also saying that he will not let go. He will never give up. He will not stop asking. One way or another, Pharaoh must give in.

BE RELENTLESS

This approach comes to a climax with the ten plagues: water turning to blood, frogs, lice, swarms of insects, livestock disease, boils, hail, locusts, darkness, and death of the Egyptian firstborn. If taken literally, the plagues make little sense: It is impossible to imagine most of these phenomena actually occurring. However, as symbols, they are highly suggestive. From the perspective of leadership, the plagues can be seen as an escalating strategy to overcome Pharaoh's intransigence. They also serve as a metaphor for Moses' refusal to relent. When one strategy does not work, another is initiated, each more powerful than the former.

Some commentators read the plagues as representations of the various gods of ancient Egypt. Turning the lifeblood of Egypt—the Nile—into actual blood is a strike against the god Hopi, the spirit of the Nile; the frog infestation could be construed as an attack on Hekt, who headed up one of Egypt's oldest fertility cults; the winged pestilence might be tied to the scarab-headed god Khephera; the killing of Egypt's cattle to Hathor, the cow-headed love goddess, and of course, Pharaoh himself is often referred to as a bull. Boils could be an out-and-out attack on Im-Hotep, the healer who becomes helpless in the face of the suffering Egyptians; the hail could be associated with Nut, goddess of the sky; the thick darkness with defeat of Amon-Ra, the sun god; and the death of the firstborn could symbolically suggest the end of Egyptian dynastic power.

For leaders, the message is clear. Before the birth of something new, the old, corrupt system must die. Moses knows this. And he knows he must stay the course, not stopping until the old order has met its demise. What is troubling here is the suffering of innocents; but again, when read as metaphor, the story teaches us that while some may be spared for a period, eventually oppression directed at some becomes the problem of all.

CELEBRATE MILESTONES

Then Miriam the prophetess, Aaron's sister, took a timbrel in her hand, and all the women went out after her in dance with timbrels. And Miriam chanted for them:

Sing to the LORD, for He has triumphed gloriously;

Horse and driver He has hurled into the sea. (Exodus 15:20–21)

The first thing the people of Israel do when the waters of the sea close behind them, drowning the Egyptian army and making their escape final and complete, is break into song. There are many things that could come before the song. They could set up tents, arrange themselves into groups, figure out what to do next, feed their children, count up their gold and silver. But all those things can wait. Instead, they begin to sing, first led by Moses, and then Miriam. This suggests that art, beauty, creativity, and emotion are as important as ideology and practical strategies.

PLAN FOR COMPLAINTS AND INSURRECTION

In the wilderness, the whole Israelite community grumbled against Moses and Aaron. The Israelites said to them, "If only we had died by the hand of the LORD in the land of Egypt, when we sat by the fleshpots, when we ate our fill of bread! For you have brought us into this wilderness to starve this whole congregation to death." (Exodus 16:2–3)

No sooner are the children of Israel released from their bondage than they begin to complain. They are free but they are hungry, and panic makes them irrational. With easily recognizable human forgetfulness, they focus only on the "fleshpots" of Egypt, and do not remember their misery and despair. One of the most striking characteristics of the biblical text as a whole is the centrality of complaint. Judaism is not interested in asceticism and self-denial, and rejects the idea of martyrdom based on forbearance. This is a remarkable phenomenon, and one that often distinguishes Jewish culture from its Christian counterparts. Jews are not only allowed to complain; they are encouraged to complain.

Complaining is a Jewish pastime, and one that is deeply ingrained. Its origins are biblical. Not only here, but throughout the biblical narrative, complaints are perceived as natural and necessary. The prophets complain that the people are not following the faith. Abraham complains to God. Moses complains about his task. Women complain to their husbands.

And now, when the children of Israel despair, the same acceptance of their complaints is shown, and a solution, in the form of sustenance pouring down from the heavens (the substance known as manna), is provided.

Why are grievance and complaint so important in the Bible and in Judaism? The answer is in a way quite simple. The word "grievance" is tied to the word "grief"; complaint arises from a sense of deep dissatisfaction. Without complaint, there is no criticism, and without criticism there is no vision of the way things can be. Complaint is the beginning of the vision of a better world. It rejects complacency and it rejects acceptance of the status quo. As a leader, Moses understands this. He understands the fear, anger, and ingratitude that results in the grumbling of the people, but he also understands that complaining is natural and necessary.

The situation is repeated soon after the manna begins to fall. The people continue to grumble, asking why Moses brought them from Egypt only to kill them, their children, and their cattle with thirst. Moses calls out to the Lord, fearing that the people are so angry they are ready to stone him.

Once again, the people are not chastised. And Moses becomes a complainer too. As the people are grumbling to him, he grumbles to God. How human he sounds when he asks, like an exasperated parent, what should he do with these children who might kill him at any moment? Instead of focusing on the complainers, God once again offers a solution: If Moses hits the stone before him, water will be released.

The message for leaders is embedded in the attitude toward these complaints: Don't allow complaint and grumbling to hold you back. Strike the rock—take action—and water will appear.

DEMAND MORAL EXCELLENCE

Moses came down from the mountain to the people and warned the people to stay pure, and they washed their clothes. And he said to the people, "Be ready for the third day: do not go near a woman."

On the third day, as morning dawned, there was thunder, and lightning, and a dense cloud upon the mountain, and a very loud blast of the horn; and all the people who were in the camp trembled. Moses led the people out of the camp toward God, and they took their places at the foot of the mountain.

Now Mount Sinai was all in smoke, for the LORD had come down upon it in fire; the smoke rose like the smoke of a kiln, and the whole mountain trembled violently. The blare of the horn grew louder and louder. As Moses spoke, God answered him in thunder. The LORD came down upon Mount Sinai, on the top of the mountain, and Moses went up. (Exodus 19:14–20)

We come now to the climax of the deliverance narrative: God hands Moses the Ten Commandments, or, according to tradition, the Torah. The first question that comes to mind is why this event is so climactic and why it is described with such powerful, unforgettable imagery. What is it about the ascension to Mount Sinai that stirs our imagination and makes the image of Moses holding the tablets iconic and essential?

What Moses is giving the people is a purpose, a guide, an explanation, a place in history, a way to live, a reason for choosing this form of life, a spiritual identity, an inspiration for faith, and above all a massive transformation from lawlessness and chaos to a society organized by principles and beliefs. The event itself is surrounded by ritual. These rituals of holiness serve to prepare the people for the magnitude of these events and the significance of what they are about to receive. They have witnessed many miracles: the plagues, the passing over of their houses, the parting of the waters, manna from the skies, water from a rock, a pillar of fire at night and a pillar of smoke during the day.

Yet they must be made to understand, and the story must make us understand, that these were all preliminaries and in a sense pragmatic events. From an allegorical point of view, the miracles that came up to now show us that where there is a will to bring about redemption and deliverance, there will be a way to do it.

But now we are in the presence of a very different and very mysterious reality. The people are about to experience something utterly holy and special, like no other thing that ever was or ever would be again. Here is the heart of Israel, the heart of our existence.

The description of the giving of the Torah is deeply moving, and the language becomes infused with poetic power. The climax of the narrative is the linking of law and freedom, of justice and human dignity.

All great leaders understand that they are subject to human limitations. Dictatorship is an effort to take on divine attributes: The dictator assumes a position of omnipotence and omnipresence (through secret police) and believes that this godlike position can be sustained. But a true leader is not a dictator and never will be. A leader understands that humans are all equal, and he or she never strives for the complete subordination of everyone else.

This is the true nature of the covenant. It is not an arbitrary set of rules and the promise of support in exchange for obedience. Nor is it an injunction to create thousands of additional rules. Rather, we are meant to move beyond such fundamentalist approaches and to see in the covenant a thrilling pact: Live as good people, according to principles of compassion, justice, and equality, and you will be rewarded by your own sense of spiritual fulfillment, your sense of the beauty of mystery, your loving closeness to others, your knowledge that you have changed the world for the better.

ANTICIPATE BACKSLIDING

When the people saw that Moses was so long in coming down from the mountain, the people gathered against Aaron and said to him, "Come, make us a god who shall go before us, for that man Moses, who brought us from the land of Egypt—we do not know what has happened to him." (Exodus 32:1)

Moses cannot be in two places at once. While he is receiving the laws, he must leave Aaron in charge. But Aaron too needs Moses, and without Moses' leadership, he is lost. Doubts begin to fill the people and they turn to Aaron. "That man Moses"— this random, unknown person—has suddenly vanished.

This brings us back to the emphasis on remembering. Humans have short memories and frequently forget the good that others have done as soon as obstacles arise. The irony of the text is not lost on the reader. The story makes us see with disbelief and astonishment the ingratitude of the people. And yet we can see ourselves in these all too human flaws. It is for this reason that we must repeat the story of the Exodus every year; not only to remind ourselves of the centrality of justice and deliverance, but also to remind ourselves of our own shortcomings.

The people slide easily from doubt toward idolatry and create the golden calf. This image is potent when read as a metaphor for overvaluing material things. Just as the children of Israel are accustomed to idolatry—as they were familiar with it in Egypt—so we can easily be drawn into a world of endless consumerism, addictions, and meaningless distractions. In this universal story, every human tendency is addressed, and we may see ourselves reflected every step of the way.

PASS ON THE MANTLE

Then Moses called Joshua and said to him in the sight of all Israel: "Be strong and resolute, for it is you who shall go with this people into the land that the LORD swore to their fathers to give them, and it is you who shall apportion it to them. And the LORD Himself will go before you. He will be with you; He will not fail or forsake you. Fear not and be not dismayed!" (Deuteronomy 31:7–8)

The image of the mantle, which is taken from the story of Elijah's death and the transfer of his mantle onto his disciple

Elisha's shoulders, is a crucial one and brings to life a saying traditionally attributed to Rabbi Tarfon: "It is not for you to complete the task but neither are you free to disengage from it" (*Pirkei Avot* 2:21).

Moses may not complete the task, but he never disengages from it. Even when criticized, defeated, and tired, even when angry and disappointed, he stays the course and brings the Hebrews to the Promised Land.

Every leader reaches a point in his life when he realizes that it is time for the next generation to take over. In an unusual reference to a character's state of health in old age, the text informs us that Moses, though old, had lost neither his sight nor his mental acuity. Nevertheless, the time has come for him to pass the mantle of leadership over to Joshua.

This is as it should be. Every quest has different stages, and Moses, given his far-reaching vision of the Promised Land, understands that he does not have the skills needed for the next stage. Moses knows he would be one important link in a whole chain of people needed to create a just nation. Wisely, he passes the mantle to Joshua.

As a leader, it is never easy to pass the torch to the next generation. Some leaders are never able to do this, and that is not good for a company or a project. I am fortunate not to count myself among those, as I take the deepest of pleasure in watching the next generation take up the Jewish call to bring justice and greater humaneness to the world.

These include my own children and grandchildren. My

sons Adam and Matthew choose to work directly with the Jewish world, while others in my family engage in the broader humanistic arena. My daughter Holly seeks to serve the needs of impoverished Indian farmers through her company Organic India; my grandson Benjamin Bronfman serves as a principal and associate managing director at Global Thermostat, a company that utilizes the low-cost process heat left over in a range of industrial activities to capture carbon from the air. I am equally proud of my other children and grandchildren, who are committed, each in their ways, to the betterment of the world we all share.

I have also been in the unique position to see the young people from the Bronfman Fellowships take up the call. I am confident that their work will have a positive impact on the world, and I am grateful for the role I have been able to play in nurturing this new group of leaders.

UNDERSTANDING THE END IS A BEGINNING

Moses went up from the steppes of Moab to Mount Nebo, to the summit of Pisgah, opposite Jericho, and the LORD showed him the whole land—Gilead as far as Dan; all of Naphtali; all the land of Ephraim and Manasseh; the whole land of Judah as far as the Western Sea, the Negeb; and the Plain—the Valley of Jericho, the city of palm trees—as far as Zoar. And the LORD said to him, "This is the land of which I swore to Abraham, Isaac and Jacob, 'I will assign it to your offspring.' I have let you see it with your eyes, but you will not cross there."

So Moses the servant of the LORD died there, in the land of Moab, at the command of the LORD. He buried him in the valley of the land of Moab, at the valley opposite Beth-peor, and no one knows his burial place to this day. Moses was a hundred and twenty years old when he died; his eyes were undimmed and his vigor unabated. And the Israelites bewailed Moses in the steppes of Moab for thirty days. (Deuteronomy 34:1–8)

The Five Books of Moses begin with Creation. The words sweep us into a poetic description of the mysterious beginning of the universe: light from the abyss, order from chaos. The final verses of the Torah are equally unforgettable, as they describe the death and burial of Judaism's greatest prophet.

What are the reasons for ending the Torah with the death of Moses? And why was Moses not allowed into the Promised Land, after leading his people through the desert for forty years?

In the Bible, God refers to generalized, nonspecific transgressions when he tells Moses that he cannot enter the land of Canaan (Deuteronomy 32:51). The judgment remains enigmatic. And so in *midrash* after *midrash*, our sages suggest different possibilities that, though varied, generally try to draw a link between Moses' behavior and the "punishment" of not entering the land.

Yet is it a punishment? I feel that these commentators are looking at the wrong part of the story. The emphasis should really be on what Moses does experience before he dies. On Mount Nebo, he sees the entire Promised Land. The extensive naming of the places in front of him tells us this is not a brief glimpse, but a deep, all-encompassing vision. It would not really be possible to see the entire land of Canaan from the top of the mountain. Instead, God is showing Moses the future that is really what most leaders want: They want to know that their dreams and vision will live on.

I would gather from everything we know about Moses that after his initial disappointment, he is at peace with the verdict of nonentry. He cannot have everything; he cannot lead forever; nor, I speculate, does he really believe he can be everything to everyone.

But I also wonder why the Torah did not end here, or with the now familiar admonitions to obey the law or the formulaic reiteration of the nature of the covenant, or even with a paean to God. Instead, we are told, in the simplest possible manner, of the great prophet's death.

In doing this, I think the biblical writers wanted us to understand that Moses' was a very ordinary death, for in the end, all death is ordinary. They wanted us to understand that in his corporeality, Moses is no different from any other human being.

He is, the final verses of the Torah make clear, the greatest of all prophets:

> Never again did there arise in Israel a prophet like Moses—whom the LORD singled out, face to face, for the various signs and portents that the LORD sent him to display in the land of Egypt, against the Pharaoh and all his courtiers and his whole country, and for all the great might and awesome power that Moses displayed before all Israel. (Deuteronomy 34:10–12)

But Moses is human; he is not a god. That his grave remains unknown prevents the possibility of a shrine, which might encourage the worshipping of him. This absence turns our eyes toward his teachings—the great laws he passed on that showed us that freedom and responsibility are inextricably linked.

Not surprisingly, the last word of the Torah is "Israel." It seems to me that we are being told that the commitment to Israel—the people—must be the focus, not Moses.

And since "Israel" means "wrestling with God," the Torah also seems to charge the Jewish people with the task of "wrestling," a term I take to mean a commitment to struggling with that which we find difficult to embrace and not letting go until we find the truths we seek.

According to Jewish tradition, every man, woman, and child—both those present and those yet unborn—stood together at Sinai when the great gift of the Torah was given. Another *midrash*, equally powerful, describes how the mountain rose up over the gathered assembly forming a *huppah*, a wedding canopy, as a symbol of the marriage between human beings and God. I understand this as a wedding between the people and godliness: the best parts of our nature and the most developed parts of our consciousness.

Just as important as the great gift of moral and ethical laws was the fact that it was presented to the whole nation, not just a single individual or small group of initiates. This was a gift for the people, not just priests or leaders or kings. Thus the nation became holy. Judaism is absolutely unique in this.

———

I end where I began, with Einstein's quote: "The pursuit of knowledge for its own sake, an almost fanatical love of justice, and the desire for personal independence—these are the features of the Jewish tradition which make me thank my stars I belong to it."

Like Einstein, I thank my stars that I have been privileged to be born into this tradition, a tradition that right from the start reminds us that we can rise above the circumstances of our birth, a tradition that, even in the face of death, never wavered in its commitment to life—this life, here on earth.

Like Einstein, I thank my stars I have been privileged to be born into a tradition that cherishes family, community, and education; a tradition that boldly put forth the notion that freedom and responsibility are inextricably bound; a tradition that champions the questioner and doesn't scorn the doubter; a tradition rich with rogues and rebels and outright revolutionaries who more often than not went on to become the heroes of history.

Like Einstein, I thank my stars that I have been privileged to be born into a tradition that asserts that deed is more important than creed; a tradition that gave the world fierce-eyed prophets who thirsted for justice and who, like Isaiah, sang out lines of moving poetry that even now, thousands of years later, continue to resonate in our hearts:

> Thus He will judge among the nations
> And arbitrate for the many peoples,
> And they shall beat their swords into ploughshares
> And their spears into pruning hooks;
> Nation shall not take up
> Sword against nation;
> They shall never again know war.
>   (Isaiah 2:4)

Like Einstein, I thank my stars that I was born into a people who, despite being one of the most hounded in history, have retained their incurable sense of humor; a people who never stopped believing that life is so infinitely precious that, as the Talmudic saying goes, "whosoever saves a single life, saves an entire universe" (Mishnah Sanhedrin 4:5).

I have given much of my life to the Jewish world, and wish I had many more years to serve this noble calling. But everything has its natural end, and so now, as my time on earth draws to a close, I would thank my stars even more if you would choose to stand at Sinai; if you would choose, as I did so many years ago, to join this remarkable people who generation after generation held fast to the dream that through our individual and collective efforts we could transform the troubled world we share into a more perfect, more humane, more civilized place.

Selah.

ACKNOWLEDGMENTS

Edgar M. Bronfman's *Why Be Jewish?* grew from conversation and collaboration with many people who embraced his vision and helped bring it into the world.

Two individuals deserve special thanks for their pivotal role in shaping the book. Margaret Wolfson, a dear friend and scribe, brought her storytelling talents and fierce dedication. Ruth Andrew Ellenson, gifted journalist, writer, and editor, was crucial in developing the book's concept and ideas.

Thank you to Beth Zasloff, who co-wrote an earlier book with Edgar and who, because of her years of collaboration with him, made the final edits on the manuscript in a way no one else could. Beloved sister Phyllis Lambert offered a deep and nuanced reading of an early draft of the manuscript. Neri Zilber contributed valuable research. Pinchas Shapiro provided critical guidance on structure. Maya Rosen conducted a detailed check of the book's sources, and Rebecca Berger advised on publicity and marketing.

Dan Mandel is an agent of true talent and vision who has offered tremendous advocacy every step of the way. *Why Be Jewish?* could not have found a better home than Twelve, a publisher dedicated to books that matter. Thank you to Sean Desmond, Brian McLendon, Bob Castillo, Libby Burton, Roland Ottewell, and Paul Samuelson for believing in the book and the conversations it aims to spark.

Carolyn Hessel and the Jewish Book Council have provided invaluable support and continue to do wonderful work to promote books that reflect the breadth of the Jewish experience.

Andy Bachman was a beloved study-partner and friend whose vision for a dynamic Jewish life and series of study sessions informed Edgar's writing, particularly on rebels in Jewish text. Edgar treasured his one-on-one sessions in philosophy with Colin Marshall, whose teaching provided important material. Michah Gottlieb worked with Edgar in a personalized, transformative study of philosophy and modern Jewish thought, and he brought his insight and expertise in reading an early draft of the manuscript. The teaching and music of Angela Warnick Buchdahl, who composed the foreword, were vital to the book's spirit.

Over a hundred dynamic and brilliant teachers from across the religious spectrum led the weekly Talmud study sessions that

Edgar convened at The Samuel Bronfman Foundation. These teachers are too many to name here, but all deserve thanks for their crucial role in fostering the lively exchange and rich text study that ground this book. Thanks are also due to the countless Hillel students at colleges in the United States and around the world with whom Edgar learned, whose observations and energy were a constant source of inspiration for him.

The Bronfman Fellowships, the diverse community of outstanding young Jews he established in 1987, gave Edgar immeasurable pride. Its extraordinary leaders—Ned Foss, Rebecca Voorwinde, and Mishael Zion—have offered support, feedback, and friendship at all stages of the writing process. Special thanks to Mishael Zion, whose comments on the manuscript integrated his deep knowledge of Jewish text and his close connection to Edgar's life, work and vision.

Edgar felt tremendous gratitude and respect for the talented and dedicated staff of The Samuel Bronfman Foundation, who for over a decade have given of themselves to create a vital center of learning, exchange, and innovation. "We are really making a difference," he told his staff at their final lunch together. Thank you to Ariel Groveman Weiner, Leigh Garofalow, and all the members of the Foundation's staff over the years for the joy and meaning they brought to Edgar's life and work.

This book would not have been possible without the passion and perseverance of Dana Raucher, executive director of The Samuel Bronfman Foundation. For over a decade, she worked with Edgar M. Bronfman to foster a renaissance in Jewish life. As the book's shepherd and advocate, she has ensured a meaningful life for the questions it asks and conversations it will begin.

Why Be Jewish? has at its heart an expression of Edgar M. Bronfman's love for his family: Jan Aronson, his life partner and thought partner; his seven children; twenty-four grandchildren; and three great-grandchildren. May his memory be a blessing.

WORKS CITED

Blake, William. "Jerusalem." In *William Blake: The Complete Illuminated Books*. New York: Thames & Hudson, 2001.

Bodian, Miriam. "Doña Gracia Nasi." In *Jewish Women: A Comprehensive Historical Encyclopedia*. March 1, 2009. Jewish Women's Archive. http://jwa.org/encyclopedia/article/nasi-dona-gracia.

Bronfman, Edgar M. *The Bronfman Hagaddah*. New York: Rizzoli International, 2013.

Brooks, Geraldine. "What Does It Mean to Be a Jew Today? What Do Jews Bring to the World Today?" *Moment*, May–June 2010. http://www.momentmag.com/moment-asks-35-american-jews-two-big-questions-what-does-it-mean-to-be-a-jew-today-what-do-jews-bring-to-the-world-today/2.

Calderon, Ruth. "The Time Has Come to Re-appropriate What Is Ours." *Jewish Week*, May 29, 2013.

Einstein, Albert. "Science and Religion." http://www.sacred-texts.com/aor/einstein/einsci.htm.

———. *The World as I See It*. London: Bodley Head, 1935.

"Einstein Believes in 'Spinoza's God.'" *New York Times*, April 25, 1929.

Emerson, Ralph Waldo. *The Essential Writings of Ralph Waldo Emerson*. New York: Modern Library Classics, 2000.

Goodstein, Laurie. "Bar Mitzvahs Get New Looks to Build Faith." *New York Times*, September 3, 2013.

Gould, Stephen Jay. *Dinosaur in a Haystack: Reflections in Natural History*. New York: Three Rivers Press, 1995.

Heschel, Abraham Joshua. "No Religion Is an Island." In *Moral Grandeur and Spiritual Audacity*. Edited by Susannah Heschel. New York: Farrar, Straus & Giroux, 1996.

————. *The Sabbath*. New York: Farrar, Straus & Giroux, 1951.

Hyman, Paula E. "Bat Mitzvah: American Jewish Women." In *Jewish Women: A Comprehensive Historical Encyclopedia*. March 1, 2009. Jewish Women's Archive. http://jwa.org/encyclopedia/article/bat-mitzvah-american-jewish-women.

The Jewish Bible: Tanakh; The Holy Scriptures—The New JPS Translation According to the Traditional Hebrew Text. Philadelphia: Jewish Publication Society of America, 1985.

The Jewish Innovation Economy: An Emerging Market for Knowledge and Social Capital. Los Angeles and New York: Jumpstart, the Natan Fund, and The Samuel Bronfman Foundation, 2011.

Kaplan, Mordecai. *Dynamic Judaism: The Essential Writings of Mordecai M. Kaplan*. Edited by Emanuel S. Goldsmith and Mel Scult. New York: Fordham University Press, 1985.

Kirsch, Adam. "A Talmudic Journey Begins," *Tablet*, August 7, 2012. http://tabletmag.com/jewish-life-and-religion/108518/a-talmudic-journey-begins.

Maimonides, Moses. *The Guide of the Perplexed*. Translated by Shlomo Pines. Chicago: University of Chicago Press, 1963.

"Marriage Project." Keshet. https://www.keshetonline.org/resources/marriage-project.

Mendelssohn, Moses. *Jerusalem: Or on Religious Power and Judaism.* Translated by Allan Arkush. Waltham, MA: Brandeis University Press, 1983.

Novak, William. "A Conversation with Michael Paley." *Kerem*, January 2011.

Pogrebin, Abigail. "High Holiday Services Are Boring. Here's How We Can Fix Them." *Tablet*, August 27, 2013. http://www.tabletmag.com/jewish-life-and-religion/142250/boring-high-holiday-services.

"Prof. Einstein Praises Effort to Make Talmud More Accessible." December 31, 1930. JTA. http://www.jta.org/1930/12/31/archive/prof-einstein-praises-effort-to-make-talmud-accessible.

"Rabbi Sharon Brous Extended Interview." *Religion and Ethics Newsweekly*, April 15, 2011. http://www.pbs.org/wnet/religionandethics/2011/04/15/april-15-2011-rabbi-sharon-brous-extended-interview/8591.

Schulweis, Harold. "Outreach to Jewish Secularists and Atheists." Valley Beth Shalom (Encino, CA), Yom Kippur 2004. http://www.vbs.org/page.cfm?p=742.

———. "Morality: The Duty to Disobey." *Reform Judaism*, Spring 2009.

Spinoza, Benedict de. *Ethics*. New York: Penguin Classics, 2005.

Wiesel, Elie. *Messengers of God: Biblical Portraits and Legends*. New York: Touchstone, 1976.

Wolf, Arnold Jacob. *The Condition of Jewish Belief: A Symposium*. Compiled by the editors of *Commentary*. New York: Macmillan, 1966.

Wordsworth, William. *The Major Works, Including "The Prelude."* Oxford: Oxford World's Classics, 2008.

INDEX

ABOUT THE AUTHOR

Edgar M. Bronfman was a businessman, statesman, and philanthropist who led historic achievements for the Jewish people and, in his later years, sought to inspire a "renaissance" in Jewish life.

As longtime CEO of Seagram Company Ltd., he directed the company to prominence and expansion throughout the world and across several industries. Using his skills and platform as a businessman, he served for over twenty years as President of the World Jewish Congress, where he worked to right grievous wrongs and to build better relations with other religions. Among his accomplishments are securing freedom and rights for Soviet Jews and winning restitution for families of Holocaust victims.

As a philanthropist, he found new ways to engage Jewish youth in their heritage and prepare them to be future leaders. He was founding Chairman of the Board of Governors of Hillel: The Foundation for Jewish Campus Life. Through The Samuel Bronfman Foundation, he nurtured initiatives that cultivate Jewish learning and pluralism, including Hillel:

The Foundation for Jewish Campus Life, The Bronfman Fellowships, and MyJewishLearning, Inc.

He is the recipient of numerous honors and awards, including the Presidential Medal of Freedom, the highest civilian honor of the United States.

Edgar M. Bronfman passed away in December of 2013, survived by his wife, Jan Aronson, his seven children, twenty-three grandchildren, and three great-grandchildren. He completed *Why Be Jewish?*, his sixth book, during his final months. He wrote the book in the hope that his own story would inspire a younger generation to delve into the Jewish tradition and bring it new life.